New Da

Edited by **Sally Welch**

May–August 2017

The Bible Reading Fellowship
15 The Chambers, Vineyard
Abingdon OX14 3FE
brf.org.uk

The Bible Reading Fellowship (BRF) is a Registered Charity (233280)

ISBN 978 0 85746 443 9
All rights reserved

This edition © The Bible Reading Fellowship 2017

Cover image and illustration on page 141 © Thinkstock

Distributed in Australia by:
MediaCom Education Inc, PO Box 610, Unley, SA 5061
Tel: 1 800 811 311 | admin@mediacom.org.au

Distributed in New Zealand by:
Scripture Union Wholesale, PO Box 760, Wellington
Tel: 04 385 0421 | suwholesale@clear.net.nz

Acknowledgements
The New Revised Standard Version of the Bible, Anglicised Edition, copyright © 1989,
1995 by the Division of Christian Education of the National Council of the Churches of
Christ in the USA. Used by permission. All rights reserved.

The Holy Bible, New International Version, Anglicised edition, copyright © 1979,
1984, 2011 by Biblica. Used by permission of Hodder & Stoughton Publishers, an
Hachette UK company. All rights reserved. 'NIV' is a registered trademark of Biblica.
UK trademark number 1448790.

The Good News Bible published by The Bible Societies/HarperCollins Publishers Ltd,
UK © American Bible Society 1966, 1971, 1976, 1992, used with permission.

The Holy Bible, English Standard Version, published by HarperCollins Publishers,
© 2001 Crossway Bibles, a division of Good News Publishers. Used by permission.
All rights reserved.

The Revised Standard Version of the Bible, copyright © 1946, 1952, 1971 by the
Division of Christian Education of the National Council of the Churches of Christ in the
United States of America. Used by permission. All rights reserved.

Extracts from the Authorised Version of the Bible (The King James Bible), the rights in
which are vested in the Crown, are reproduced by permission of the Crown's Patentee,
Cambridge University Press.

The Revised Common Lectionary is copyright © The Consultation on Common Texts,
1992 and is reproduced with permission. *The Christian Year: Calendar, Lectionary and
Collects*, which includes the *Common Worship* lectionary (the Church of England's
adaptations of the *Revised Common Lectionary*, published as the Principal Service
lectionary) is copyright © The Central Board of Finance of the Church of England,
1995, 1997, and material from it is reproduced with permission.

Printed by Gutenberg Press, Tarxien, Malta

Suggestions for using *New Daylight*

Find a regular time and place, if possible, where you can read and pray undisturbed. Before you begin, take time to be still and perhaps use the BRF Prayer on page 6. Then read the Bible passage slowly (try reading it aloud if you find it over-familiar), followed by the comment. You can also use *New Daylight* for group study and discussion, if you prefer.

The prayer or point for reflection can be a starting point for your own meditation and prayer. Many people like to keep a journal to record their thoughts about a Bible passage and items for prayer. In *New Daylight* we also note the Sundays and some special festivals from the Church calendar, to keep in step with the Christian year.

New Daylight and the Bible

New Daylight contributors use a range of Bible versions, and you will find a list of the versions used opposite. You are welcome to use your own preferred version alongside the passage printed in the notes. This can be particularly helpful if the Bible text has been abridged.

New Daylight affirms that the whole of the Bible is God's revelation to us, and we should read, reflect on and learn from every part of both Old and New Testaments. Usually the printed comment presents a straightforward 'thought for the day', but sometimes it may also raise questions rather than simply providing answers, as we wrestle with some of the more difficult passages of Scripture.

New Daylight is also available in a deluxe edition (larger format). Visit your local Christian bookshop or contact the BRF office, who can also give details about a cassette version for the visually impaired. For a Braille edition, contact St John's Guild, Sovereign House, 12–14 Warwick Street, Coventry CV5 6ET.

Comment on *New Daylight*

To send feedback, you may email or write to BRF at the addresses shown opposite. If you would like your comment to be included on our website, please email connect@brf.org.uk. You can also Tweet to @brfonline (please use the hashtag #brfconnect).

Writers in this issue

Amy Boucher Pye is an American who has lived in the UK for over a decade. She makes her home in North London with her husband and young family and enjoys writing for Christian magazines.

John Twisleton is Rector of Horsted Keynes in Sussex. He writes on prayer and apologetics, broadcasts on Premier Radio, and is the author of *Meet Jesus* (BRF, 2011) and *Using the Jesus Prayer* (BRF, 2014).

Barbara Mosse is a retired Anglican priest with experience in various chaplaincies. A freelance lecturer and retreat giver, she is the author of *Welcoming the Way of the Cross* (BRF, 2013).

Peter Waddell is an Anglican priest and vicar in the Diocese of St Albans. Originally from Northern Ireland, he served for eleven years in university chaplaincy before moving into parish ministry. He is the author of *Joy: The meaning of the sacraments* (Canterbury Press, 2012).

Tim Heaton is an Anglican priest in parish ministry in north Dorset. He is the author of two Lent courses: *The Naturalist and the Christ* (Circle Books, 2011) and *The Long Road to Heaven* (Circle Books, 2013).

Helen Julian CSF is an Anglican Franciscan sister, currently serving her community as Minister General. She has written three books for BRF, including *Living the Gospel* and *The Road to Emmaus*.

Michael Mitton is Fresh Expressions Adviser for Derby Diocese, NSM Priest-in-charge of St Paul's Derby and honorary Canon of Derby Cathedral. He is the author of *Travellers of the Heart* (BRF, 2013).

John Ryeland is ordained in the Church of England and is the Director of The Christian Healing Mission. He has written several books, including *Encountering the God who Heals* (Verite CM, 2013). His focus is to encourage people to experience the presence of the healing Jesus, which so often transforms lives.

Penelope Wilcock writes Christian fiction, pastoral theology and Bible study. Her books include *Spiritual Care of Dying and Bereaved People* (BRF, 2013). She blogs at http://kindredofthequietway.blogspot.co.uk.

Sally Welch writes…

In my conversations with *New Daylight* readers I have discovered that there are many different ways in which this little book is used. For most, *New Daylight* is part of their daily prayer life, given a set time and space within the routine of the day. Even within this, however, there is variation—some people like to read through an entire fortnight's notes in one go, to get a sense of the overall theme of the studies. They then go back to the beginning and study one day at a time, keeping the context of each day within the whole. Others like to greet each individual study as a separate entity, regarding it as complete in itself. For some, however, the opportunity to sit and read comes infrequently and at unspecified intervals, so they must pick up their copy and read and reflect with great concentration. Still others prefer to take a theme once a week, studying all the passages in one go. All these approaches are valid: what is important is that we read the Bible and study God's word as regularly as we can, allowing the wisdom in this book to become part of the very core of our being.

As part of our offerings to you in this issue of *New Daylight*, you will find Amy Boucher Pye exploring the vision of Revelation, both challenging and exciting as we enter the world of John's vision. Michael Mitton introduces us to Moses once more—a man who leads his people faithfully through the wilderness, encountering difficulties and temptations, discovering much about himself and his faith. Tim Heaton shares his understanding of Paul's letter to the Philippians as a 'letter of joy'.

As well as studies focused on the Bible itself, you will find Helen Julian's investigation of the life and character of Hildegard of Bingen, showing how our understanding of faith can be expanded not just by reading the Bible but by learning from the insights of those who have gone before. And at the heart of all these contributions is a passion to discover more about the good news of Christ's saving message and its implications for us as individuals, as members of our communities and as a whole people of God.

Sally Ann Welch

The BRF Prayer

Almighty God,
you have taught us that your word is a lamp for our feet
and a light for our path. Help us, and all who prayerfully
read your word, to deepen our fellowship with you
and with each other through your love.
And in so doing may we come to know you more fully,
love you more truly, and follow more faithfully
in the steps of your son Jesus Christ, who lives and reigns
with you and the Holy Spirit, one God for evermore.
Amen

The vision of Revelation 5—22

Last November, Veronica Zundel took us through the first four chapters of Revelation, and as I started to read my assigned chapters, 5 to 22, I began to wonder if I had drawn the short straw. After all, images of hail and sulphur and woes and the great beast flashed before my eyes. But I knew too that we would reach the glorious end of the book, where the new Jerusalem is unveiled and we are invited to dwell with God for ever. There, I remembered, we'd find jewels and light and fine linen and living water.

The book of Revelation is famously hard to comprehend, but if we try to view it from the point of view of the early church to whom it was written, we can deepen our understanding. For instance, it is the New Testament book that draws the most from Old Testament books, especially Ezekiel and Daniel, and the early church believers would have been familiar with these references. The apocalyptic visions we see in these Old Testament books are often fulfilled in John's vision of the end times.

But it's not only a book for the early church; it's for us in the 21st century to delve into in the hope of deepening our understanding of the age to come. Although in Revelation we see many of God's judgements against those who refuse to bow their knees to him, we also find his invitation to drink the water that will satisfy our thirst for ever. We can find images to ponder and chew over, that our imaginations would be filled with all that is good, true and beautiful. Doing the practice of sacred reading—*lectio divina*—with a section of Revelation 21, for example, will bear fruit as the words sink into our beings.

To help me understand the series of sevens—scrolls, trumpets and bowls—and other symbols, I've had the help of the *NIV Application Commentary: Revelation* by Craig Kenner (Zondervan, 2000).

May you gain in your love for God as you read from this revelation of things to come. Come, Lord Jesus.

AMY BOUCHER PYE

Worthy is the Lamb

'Do not weep! See, the Lion of the tribe of Judah, the Root of David, has triumphed. He is able to open the scroll and its seven seals.'... Then I looked and heard the voice of many angels, numbering thousands upon thousands, and ten thousand times ten thousand... In a loud voice they were saying: 'Worthy is the Lamb, who was slain, to receive power and wealth and wisdom and strength and honour and glory and praise!' Then I heard every creature in heaven and on earth and under the earth and on the sea, and all that is in them, saying: 'To him who sits on the throne and to the Lamb be praise and honour and glory and power, for ever and ever!'

We begin with worshipping the Lamb. This is appropriate, for the book of Revelation honours and exalts Jesus, whose sacrifice on the cross marks him worthy to open the scroll and the seven seals. Although some of the visions and images in this book can be difficult to interpret, we can come back to the idea that he is worthy to be praised.

All creation worships him, including an uncountable number of angels, as the 'ten thousand times ten thousand' signifies in the original Greek. So do creatures in the sea and on earth, which makes me think of fish flying out of the water, or blackbirds raising a song, or insects buzzing over the surface of a pond—all in worship. And so do women and men worship as they name the triune God as their Lord.

One catechism (a teaching document) created in the 17th century lists as its first question, what is the 'chief end' of humanity? It gives as its answer: 'to glorify God, and to enjoy him for ever'. Whether we agree with the catechism's finer points of theology, we can unite around this statement of the way we were made to worship the Lord.

May our words and deeds echo the cries of angels and all creatures, saying, 'Worthy is the Lamb!'

'You are worthy, our Lord and God, to receive glory and honour and power, for you created all things, and by your will they were created and have their being' (Revelation 4:11).

AMY BOUCHER PYE

A great multitude

After this I looked, and there before me was a great multitude that no one could count, from every nation, tribe, people and language, standing before the throne and before the Lamb. They were wearing white robes and were holding palm branches in their hands. And they cried out in a loud voice: 'Salvation belongs to our God, who sits on the throne, and to the Lamb.'... Then one of the elders asked me, 'These in white robes—who are they, and where did they come from?' I answered, 'Sir, you know.' And he said, 'These are they who have come out of the great tribulation; they have washed their robes and made them white in the blood of the Lamb.'

Living in London, I often forget my Americanness because of the large number of people from different countries who live in this city. In our church, for instance, we have 19 nationalities among the 150 who attend, and it's a foretaste of heaven. And yet, how much more glorious that will be when the great multitude who stand before the throne are too numerous to count and come from every tribe and speak every language.

Their white robes and palm branches probably hint at the Old Testament—for example, the vision of the end times given to Daniel, who learned that people would be 'purified, made spotless and refined' (Daniel 12:10) and thus made able to wear white robes, which signify purity. The palm branches could refer to the Feast of Tabernacles, which celebrated God's people's exodus from Egypt, and, of course, those who welcomed Jesus into Jerusalem on Palm Sunday. The Lord weaves his story through the generations.

Note too in this vision the cleansing and uniting work of the Lamb. As we witness the heart-wrenching scenes of bloody conflicts around the world, we can pray that God will usher in his peace and resolution. For we know that one day all tribes will stand together, and we yearn to glimpse that display of communion this side of heaven.

Lord God, we sometimes lose hope when we witness acts of atrocity, but we know that you are the God of peace. Extend your kingdom, we pray.

AMY BOUCHER PYE

The trumpet sounds

When he opened the seventh seal, there was silence in heaven for about half an hour. And I saw the seven angels who stand before God, and seven trumpets were given to them... Then the seven angels who had the seven trumpets prepared to sound them. The first angel sounded his trumpet, and there came hail and fire mixed with blood, and it was hurled down on the earth. A third of the earth was burned up, a third of the trees were burned up, and all the green grass was burned up.

Modern-day Christians may find the book of Revelation daunting and difficult, not only because it is apocalyptic literature, which can be difficult to interpret, but because of its scenes of battle and damnation. In John's vision he sees three sets of seven—seven seals, seven trumpets and seven bowls—and from them God releases his final judgement on an unbelieving world. With the sounding of each of the seven trumpets, we see plagues of hail, blood and fire released, each bringing destruction in its wake. The original reader would have connected the seven trumpets to the plagues the Lord sent on Pharaoh and the Egyptians when Moses was trying to lead God's people to the promised land.

We may recoil at the thought of judgement, but the early Christians, suffering persecution under the Roman emperor, probably found comfort and encouragement in seeing evil silenced. More recently, I've heard of Chinese Christians who looked to the book of Revelation for hope and empowerment during the Cultural Revolution under Mao Zedong. They longed for justice and for their voice to be heard. What they found in Revelation was a picture of wrongs being righted and the Judge pronouncing his verdict.

Today, perhaps consider praying for and supporting the persecuted Christians around the world whose voice may be silenced—those in North Korea, Iraq, Eritrea, Syria or Afghanistan, for instance. If you want to find out more, see the website of the Christian organisation Open Doors (opendoorsUK.org), which lists the top 50 countries of persecution.

Father God, you are the ultimate judge; you are the source of fairness and justice. Thank you that I do not have to make myself the judge and arbiter.

AMY BOUCHER PYE

Sweet and sour

'Go, take the scroll that lies open in the hand of the angel who is standing on the sea and on the land.' So I went to the angel and asked him to give me the little scroll. He said to me, 'Take it and eat it. It will turn your stomach sour, but "in your mouth it will be as sweet as honey".' I took the little scroll from the angel's hand and ate it. It tasted as sweet as honey in my mouth, but when I had eaten it, my stomach turned sour. Then I was told, 'You must prophesy again about many peoples, nations, languages and kings.'

Before the seventh angel blows the seventh trumpet, we have an interlude during which a mighty angel opens a little scroll, which many scholars think represents the book of Revelation. John is instructed to take and eat it, and although it will taste sweet in his mouth, it will turn sour in his stomach.

The Bible in several places calls God's word as sweet as honey (for example, in Psalm 19:10 and Psalm 119:103), but the early church would probably have thought of the Old Testament prophet Ezekiel here. He was called to speak to a rebellious nation—God's own people in exile. In preparation the Lord instructed him to 'eat this scroll' of words of lament and mourning, which would taste as sweet as honey (see Ezekiel 2—3). Ezekiel was faithful to his task but faced opposition. John too was to eat the scroll and proclaim its words of woe—and this time the audience would be not only the Israelites, but all peoples and nations. At the end of time, God's word will be heard by everyone.

We don't know when the end of time will come, but this passage can encourage us to 'eat the scroll' of the Bible to be ready: we can read it, meditating on its words as we chew them over so that they go deep within. Then we will be able to speak the sweet words at the opportune moment—end of time or not.

Lord God, help me to meditate on your words, so that I may be transformed by your truth and that my speech may be winsome and engaging.

AMY BOUCHER PYE

The word of their testimony

Then war broke out in heaven. Michael and his angels fought against the dragon, and the dragon and his angels fought back... The great dragon was hurled down—that ancient snake called the devil, or Satan, who leads the whole world astray... Then I heard a loud voice in heaven say: 'Now have come the salvation and the power and the kingdom of our God, and the authority of his Messiah. For the accuser of our brothers and sisters, who accuses them before our God day and night, has been hurled down. They triumphed over him by the blood of the Lamb and by the word of their testimony; they did not love their lives so much as to shrink from death.'

Stories of martyrdom resonate, partly because when we hear them we may wonder what we would do in the martyr's place. Could we stand and proclaim our love for the triune God when staring down the barrel of a gun? I pray we'll never need to find out.

We see the power of the faithfulness of the saints in this part of John's vision, which seems to pull a curtain back to reveal the great drama taking place in the heavens. Satan is defeated in his evil mission not only by Jesus' death on the cross but by the 'word of their testimony'. God triumphs, and the evil one, who accuses the saints continually, loses his place in heaven—and all his angels with him.

We can take heart that with Christ dwelling in us, we can be transformed into people who can stand against the schemes of the evil one, whatever the guise in which they appear. As we share how the Lord works in our lives, we can spread hope and encouragement to those who may wonder if God is real or still active in the world. This passage reminds us not to underestimate the power of our testimony.

'My mouth will tell of your righteous deeds, of your saving acts all day long—though I know not how to relate them all. I will come and proclaim your mighty acts, Sovereign Lord; I will proclaim your righteous deeds, yours alone' (Psalm 71:15–16).

AMY BOUCHER PYE

God's winepress

Still another angel, who had charge of the fire, came from the altar and called in a loud voice to him who had the sharp sickle, 'Take your sharp sickle and gather the clusters of grapes from the earth's vine, because its grapes are ripe.' The angel swung his sickle on the earth, gathered its grapes and threw them into the great winepress of God's wrath. They were trampled in the winepress outside the city, and blood flowed out of the press, rising as high as the horses' bridles for a distance of 1,600 stadia.

Recently I heard the story of an avowed atheist academic who, over time, became a follower of Jesus, partly through reading the work of N.T. Wright, and also through examining the thoughts of others who had travelled the same road before her, such as C.S. Lewis. When she examined the evidence for the validity of the gospel, including the existence of hell, she turned from her atheism and believed.

The preaching of fire and brimstone, however, is not something we normally embrace. After all, it would not make for polite conversation to tell someone that they might be seen as one of the grapes gathered up and thrown into the winepress, resulting in blood rising as high as the horses' bridles. I'm not advocating this approach, either, for we do not have the mind of God and are not fit to be the judge. But sometimes, even without such preaching, people are swayed to examine the reality of ultimate things such as heaven and hell. And in the scriptures we will find the tools to aid them in their search.

As the apostle Paul wrote to the church at Corinth, 'For we must all appear before the judgement seat of Christ, so that each of us may receive what is due to us for the things done while in the body, whether good or bad' (2 Corinthians 5:10). May we know the sweet assurance of the Advocate who stands in our place.

'My dear children, I write this to you so that you will not sin. But if anybody does sin, we have an advocate with the Father—Jesus Christ, the Righteous One' (1 John 2:1).

AMY BOUCHER PYE

They cursed God

Then I heard a loud voice from the temple saying to the seven angels, 'Go, pour out the seven bowls of God's wrath on the earth.'… The seventh angel poured out his bowl into the air, and out of the temple came a loud voice from the throne, saying, 'It is done!' Then there came flashes of lightning, rumblings, peals of thunder and a severe earthquake. No earthquake like it has ever occurred since mankind has been on earth, so tremendous was the quake. The great city split into three parts, and the cities of the nations collapsed… From the sky huge hailstones, each weighing about forty kilograms fell on people. And they cursed God on account of the plague of hail, because the plague was so terrible.

In the third series of sevens, we see God's seven bowls of wrath being poured out in judgement against those who will not bend their knee to him. Again the plagues of Egypt are invoked in the images of blood, sores and fire being poured out of the bowls, so again the early church would have thought back to God's protection of his people against their oppressors as they sought freedom in the promised land.

In the full description of what the seven bowls unleash, we find a line repeated, 'They refused to repent' (Revelation 16:9–11). A similar sentiment is found in verse 21: 'They cursed God.' Those who worship the beast have become hardened in their beliefs, and although they have a chance to turn from their sins and turn to God, they don't. Instead, they curse God and die.

In the light of this stark judgement, we can view this passage partly as a reminder to keep our hearts supple before the Lord, coming to him in repentance for our wrongdoing and receiving from him the forgiveness for our sins. If we do this, our lifetime of habits can result not in a hardened heart but in a countenance of worship and gratitude.

Loving Father, saving Son, comforting Spirit,
let me bow my knee to you in reverence and awe,
for you are the living God who brings life, peace and joy.

AMY BOUCHER PYE

The Lord God Almighty reigns

Then I heard what sounded like a great multitude, like the roar of rushing waters and like loud peals of thunder, shouting: 'Hallelujah! For our Lord God Almighty reigns. Let us rejoice and be glad and give him glory! For the wedding of the Lamb has come, and his bride has made herself ready. Fine linen, bright and clean, was given her to wear.' (Fine linen stands for the righteous acts of God's holy people.)... At this I fell at his feet to worship him. But he said to me, 'Don't do that! I am a fellow servant with you and with your brothers and sisters who hold to the testimony of Jesus. Worship God! For it is the Spirit of prophecy who bears testimony to Jesus.'

Are you still with me? I'll admit, it's been a hard road to travel through the woes and plagues and curses we've come across in our journey through the latter part of Revelation, but we've now reached the wedding of the Lamb where we can sigh in gratitude. For the evil one has been defeated, the Lord God reigns, and the Church prepares to become the bride, united with her bridegroom for all eternity. Hallelujah!

The bride makes herself ready, donning the fine linen that harks back to the white robes put on by the martyrs, which we saw in Revelation 6:11. Note too how the fine linen stands for the righteous acts of all God's people, not just those who died for their faith.

We saw on Friday how the Lord honours the testimony of his saints, and we can note in verse 10 how that testimony comes through the Holy Spirit who dwells within the redeemed. The angel reminds John that they are fellow created beings whom God uses to spread his glory. As this passage makes clear, we should not give up hope, for the true and living God sees our faithful words and deeds.

God of all creation, you have made us for yourself and we are grateful. May we put on your fine, clean linen as we bear testimony to your Son Jesus. We revel in our status as your beloved.

AMY BOUCHER PYE

Faithful and True

I saw heaven standing open and there before me was a white horse, whose rider is called Faithful and True. With justice he judges and wages war. His eyes are like blazing fire, and on his head are many crowns. He has a name written on him that no one knows but he himself. He is dressed in a robe dipped in blood, and his name is the Word of God. The armies of heaven were following him, riding on white horses and dressed in fine linen, white and clean. Coming out of his mouth is a sharp sword with which to strike down the nations. 'He will rule them with an iron sceptre.' He treads the winepress of the fury of the wrath of God Almighty. On his robe and on his thigh he has this name written: 'King of Kings and Lord of Lords'.

John introduces another vision with his words, 'I saw heaven standing open…' This one features the resurrected Jesus who returns as the conquering king. Note the various symbols, such as riding in on a white horse: this would be appropriate for a ruler, as white horses were seen as the best. His blazing eyes probably refer to Daniel's vision of the warrior in a great war with 'eyes like flaming torches' (Daniel 10:6). He is the king, as symbolised by the many crowns, and his robe dipped in blood may refer either to his own blood on the cross or the blood of his opponents. Much of the language here in John's vision can be found in Isaiah 63, such as the red garments from trampling the winepress: ('their blood spattered my garments', Isaiah 63:3). The saints, in contrast, wear the fine linen that we have seen previously.

How humbling to think that our Saviour and Lord wears bloodstained garments, while we are given clean and pure white linen to wear! Because of our sins and wrongdoing, we don't deserve to wear these clean clothes, for we should be dressed more like Jesus. But he went to the cross that we could be made clean.

'I will sprinkle clean water on you, and you will be clean; I will cleanse you from all your impurities and from all your idols' (Ezekiel 36:25).

AMY BOUCHER PYE

No more crying

Then I saw 'a new heaven and a new earth,' for the first heaven and the first earth had passed away, and there was no longer any sea. I saw the Holy City, the new Jerusalem, coming down out of heaven from God, prepared as a bride beautifully dressed for her husband. And I heard a loud voice from the throne saying, 'Look! God's dwelling-place is now among the people, and he will dwell with them. They will be his people, and God himself will be with them and be their God. "He will wipe every tear from their eyes. There will be no more death" or mourning or crying or pain, for the old order of things has passed away.' He who was seated on the throne said, 'I am making everything new!... To the thirsty I will give water without cost from the spring of the water of life.'

When a friend visited his mother in hospital as she neared the end of her life, she was agitated and anxious. He began to read to her from the last chapters of Revelation, and as he painted the picture of the new heaven and earth, he saw her enter into a deep sense of peace. She squeezed his hand, and his eyes brimmed with tears of joy and sorrow.

This peace reigns in John's vision, for the war is over and God dwells with his people in a time of abundance. No longer are the saints marked by tears and mourning, but they know joy as they live in the new Eden. Their thirst is slaked by the water of life, and all things are made new.

Imagine a world without death or mourning or crying or pain. Living with this picture in our minds, we can face hardship and sorrow, for we know the Lord will welcome us to this new heaven and earth one day. And not only then, but he will usher in his kingdom here on earth. His gifts of love and life are not reserved only for after we die; he wants us to enjoy them now too.

Triune God, you dwell with us and we with you. May we know your loving care and the peace that passes all understanding this day.

AMY BOUCHER PYE

A very precious jewel

'Come, I will show you the bride, the wife of the Lamb.' And he carried me away in the Spirit to a mountain great and high, and showed me the Holy City, Jerusalem, coming down out of heaven from God. It shone with the glory of God, and its brilliance was like that of a very precious jewel, like a jasper, clear as crystal… The wall was made of jasper, and the city of pure gold, as pure as glass. The foundations of the city walls were decorated with every kind of precious stone… I did not see a temple in the city, because the Lord God Almighty and the Lamb are its temple. The city does not need the sun or the moon to shine on it, for the glory of God gives it light, and the Lamb is its lamp.

Jewels and light and gold and jasper and the glory of God—all images that appear in John's vision about the gift of the Holy City. This is a gift from God, for it comes down from heaven. It shines with God's glory, which is so bright that no longer are the sun or moon needed. It's likened to a jewel, and twelve precious stones adorn the walls, which were the twelve stones represented on the high priest's breastplate as depicted in Exodus 28:17–21. Each stone represents one of the tribes of Israel. But no longer is there a temple, for the whole city is God's temple, his meeting place with his people where they dwell together for ever.

The picture of the city to come is one of abundance and glory. The Lord doesn't withhold from his people the finest jewels or other natural resources, but has them available for them to enjoy. This is not a picture of a tyrant in the sky or a taskmaster, but of a giving parent who loves us deeply. 'No good thing does he withhold' from those whom he loves (Psalm 84:11).

Lord God, soak my imagination with these images that speak of how much you love me, that I would live and move out of this knowledge and share your love with a hurting world.

AMY BOUCHER PYE

The tree of life

Then the angel showed me the river of the water of life, as clear as crystal, flowing from the throne of God and of the Lamb down the middle of the great street of the city. On each side of the river stood the tree of life, bearing twelve crops of fruit, yielding its fruit every month. And the leaves of the tree are for the healing of the nations. No longer will there be any curse. The throne of God and of the Lamb will be in the city, and his servants will serve him. They will see his face, and his name will be on their foreheads… And they will reign for ever and ever.

In the new heaven and the new earth, the redeemed will live with God and will see him face to face. Their faces will radiate his glory, as Moses' did after he had met with the Lord on the mountain for 40 days to receive the law. He had to veil his face when he came down the mountain to hide this glory from God's people, but in the new world there will be no need for veils.

This is the new Eden, and it has a river flowing through the middle, even as a river watered the garden in Eden (Genesis 2:10). The trees produce healing leaves and fruit, and are the fulfilment of Ezekiel's prophecy of leaves that do not wither and fruit that doesn't fail (Ezekiel 47:12). God's people will be nourished with his food.

My grandparents were all farmers, and their lives were marked by the daily toil of caring for the land and the animals. If they experienced drought or floods, they would suffer until the new season came with its hope of new life. I wonder if God's people will care for his vegetation in his new earth. Think about gardening without the curse—even someone without a green thumb, like me, would grow lush and fragrant plants.

'The Lord will guide you always; he will satisfy your needs in a sun-scorched land and will strengthen your frame. You will be like a well-watered garden, like a spring whose waters never fail' (Isaiah 58:11).

AMY BOUCHER PYE

The beginning and the end

'Look, I am coming soon! My reward is with me, and I will give to each person according to what they have done. I am the Alpha and the Omega, the First and the Last, the Beginning and the End… I, Jesus… am the Root and the Offspring of David, and the bright Morning Star.' The Spirit and the bride say, 'Come!' And let the one who hears say, 'Come!' Let the one who is thirsty come; and let the one who wishes take the free gift of the water of life… He who testifies to these things says, 'Yes, I am coming soon.' Amen. Come, Lord Jesus.

John's vision—and indeed our Bibles—end with this invitation from God for us to join him in the Holy City. When we don our clean, white linen, we enter the gates of the only city that will never sleep. There we will live as we worship our God, united with him and our sisters and brothers.

Note the many titles for Jesus that appear in these few lines: he is the Alpha and Omega, the First and Last, the Beginning and the End. He's the Root and the Offspring of David, the bright Morning Star. All things come from him and are given through him. He was there at the foundation of the world and is there in the city to come. He is the perfect offspring of David, the ideal king in the Old Testament, as we also see in Revelation 5:5. He is the Morning Star, the fulfilment of the promise made in Revelation 2:28 and in Numbers 24:17: 'A star will come out of Jacob.'

We're welcomed to come and drink, in words that echo the glorious invitation in Isaiah 55:1: 'Come, all you who are thirsty, come to the waters; and you who have no money, come, buy and eat!' (Isaiah 55:1). Just as we are, we come, with gratitude and joy for how the Lord beckons us. We join John in saying, 'Come, Lord Jesus.'

Loving Father, living Son, life-giving Spirit, we worship and adore you, giving thanks for your plan of redemption and new life. May we live each moment to your glory.

AMY BOUCHER PYE

Working out God's salvation:
Joshua 13—24

The second half of the book of Joshua is historical less in a modern and more in a Hebrew sense—less a chronicle and more a prophetic testimony to God's loving provision for his people. This testimony continues into the rest of the Old Testament, where we see both God's rule and his merciful overruling of his people who repeatedly throw away their chances.

Joshua 13—24 is an epilogue to the Pentateuch (Torah or Law books) which precedes it at the very start of our Bible. It speaks of a fulfilment of God's promise as the land is settled. These chapters are also a curtain-raiser to Israel's ongoing failure to respond with obedience to the Law, captured in the necessary renewal of the covenant at the end of the book.

In these reflections we see Joshua in old age and how God keeps him as his instrument. We think of the grace especially afforded to the elderly, of a passive giving way within scenarios that are ripe for God to act in them. So often, our energies are counter to God's work. Joshua means 'God is salvation'. He is a pointer to Jesus as a new Joshua, leading us not out of physical but out of spiritual servitude into 'the freedom of the glory of the children of God' (Romans 8:21).

God's saving promises are realised in active faith which, following Joshua, lays hold on and 'works out' salvation (see Philippians 2:12). We will reflect from Joshua 13—24 on salvation as promise, gift and task. Biblical places, of which there are many in this section of scripture, repeatedly speak God's word to us and there is no word of God without power. This power is for salvation and it is allied to God's all consuming holiness (Joshua 24:19). In these chapters we see God in holiness and love, in a covenant conditional on his people's obedience and yet with space to offer merciful sanctuary to sinners.

The temporary rest attained by Joshua through the settlement is picked up by the author of Hebrews as foreshadowing the eternal sabbath of heaven (Hebrews 4:8–9). The passages help us reflect on Christian faith as a journey with heavenward direction, nurtured by scripture and the cycle of sacramental worship.

JOHN TWISLETON

God's servants young and old

Now Joshua was old and advanced in years; and the Lord said to him, 'You are old and advanced in years, and very much of the land still remains to be possessed... I will myself drive them out from before the Israelites; only allot the land to Israel for an inheritance, as I have commanded you. Now therefore divide this land for an inheritance to the nine tribes and the half-tribe of Manasseh.'

The book of Joshua has something for young and old. We start all over again, in a sense, with chapter 13 structured by its editor to parallel chapter 1 addressing the young Joshua. The same promise is there from God for him, though 'old and advanced in years' (v. 1), and the brief is not now for conquest but for judicious settlement of Israel in the promised land.

As I began to read this second section of Joshua, I was reminded of my calling as a priest years ago and occasions since, when God in his faithfulness has given me a reminder. Here Joshua is reminded of the Lord's being much on his case and that of Israel, in the words 'I will myself drive [the inhabitants of the hill country] out from before the Israelites' (v. 6b). The action will be God's, and Joshua's enfeeblement is immaterial.

Effective Christian ministry is often about a passive giving way within scenarios that are ripe for God's action, so that he is given space to move in them. We might become more aware of this as we grow older and wiser. Even our Lord, so active in the Gospels, is bound and passive in his greatest work at the end of these narratives.

The book of Joshua is written primarily for devotional purposes as a reminder of God's faithfulness to Israel. We know, from elsewhere in scripture, that this story was a drawn-out process, but Joshua condenses it into a miraculous whirlwind, a great deliverance achieved by God. That achievement affirms both God's rule and his overruling of human frailty.

'Even to old age and grey hairs, O God, do not forsake me,
until I proclaim your might to all the generations to come' (Psalm 71:18).

JOHN TWISLETON

Promise, gift and task

Then Joshua blessed him, and gave Hebron to Caleb son of Jephunneh for an inheritance. So Hebron became the inheritance of Caleb son of Jephunneh the Kenizzite to this day, because he wholeheartedly followed the Lord, the God of Israel. Now the name of Hebron formerly was Kiriath-arba; this Arba was the greatest man among the Anakim. And the land had rest from war.

The book of Joshua is the sixth book of the Old Testament. It follows the so-called Pentateuch (five books), called the Law (Torah), and begins the so-called Prophets. The books from Joshua to 2 Kings are the Former Prophets, with Isaiah onwards named the Latter Prophets. To the Hebrews, though, prophecy was as much about interpreting history as about predicting the future.

We find in Joshua a revisiting and interpreting of events previously mentioned in the Pentateuch, such as the story of Caleb in Numbers 14 and Deuteronomy 1:36, where his wholeheartedness is applauded. Such a quality is effective in any age, and lack of it is presented as Israel's undoing overall. Earlier in chapter 14, we see reference to God wondrously preserving Caleb's youth, and although the land of Hebron is given to him, his action to expel the mighty Anakim is also implied.

Scripture is God's word spoken through human words. However we engage with this or any text, literally or imaginatively, we can receive insight that is relevant to our inheritance as believers. The Hebrew settlement by Caleb and the others was both gift and task. Like them, we have ground to occupy. This is facilitated by recognising God's promise and gift while being ready for a wholehearted engagement to occupy ourselves on his behalf in the place where he needs us.

History is 'His Story' and the story of God's people. It is the supreme gift of scripture to excite in us faith for a future built from God's past dealings, and with a forward momentum linked to the accompaniment of the Holy Spirit.

How does God's repeated commendation of Caleb's wholeheartedness strike you? Might prayer for this grace be timely for you or your church?

JOHN TWISLETON

No word of God without power

The lot for the tribe of the people of Judah according to their families reached southwards to the boundary of Edom, to the wilderness of Zin at the farthest south. And their southern boundary ran from the end of the Dead Sea, from the bay that faces southwards; it goes out southwards of the ascent of Akrabbim, passes along to Zin, and goes up south of Kadesh-barnea, along by Hezron, up to Addar, makes a turn to Karka, passes along to Azmon, goes out by the Wadi of Egypt, and comes to its end at the sea. This shall be your southern boundary. And the eastern boundary is the Dead Sea, to the mouth of the Jordan.

When we approach scripture with penitent hearts, open to the Holy Spirit, we are in a position to hear God's word—and there's no word of God without power!

I wonder how you're faring as you follow Joshua 13—24, with so many unfamiliar names concerning settlements made around 3000 years ago. Even though the Jewish people have survived—a great evidence of God's faithfulness—many of the places mentioned here have not. Some remain, however, and Joshua 15:1–5 lists places whose names retain spiritual significance and power evident in the Holy Land today. The Dead Sea is even more dead than in Joshua's time, so saline that you can float upon it. The River Jordan still flows north of it and the wilderness of Zin (Sin) lies deep south.

Biblical places can speak God's word to us, and these places contrast with one another. Jordan is associated with life in the Holy Spirit, as the place where the new Joshua (Jesus) was anointed as Christ to be bearer of the Spirit to those who will welcome that anointing. Sin, the lost place, and the Dead Sea remind us of situations where life has got distracted from the best course. As we turn from any such situation that we rest in here and now, acts of repentance and faith invite spiritual refreshment. We can be settled afresh in the place God wants us to be.

Lord, take me to the places you have assigned for me today. Amen

JOHN TWISLETON

Finding God's space

Then Joshua said to the house of Joseph, to Ephraim and Manasseh, 'You are indeed a numerous people, and have great power; you shall not have one lot only, but the hill country shall be yours, for though it is a forest, you shall clear it and possess it to its farthest borders; for you shall drive out the Canaanites, though they have chariots of iron, and though they are strong.'

We find in the book of Joshua a sort of epilogue to the Pentateuch which precedes it at the very start of our Bible. There's a fulfilment of what God promised and, most especially, land to be settled on, after its judicious division, for each house or tribe of Israel. Joseph's numerous house, named after his sons Ephraim and Manasseh, attains to the hill country, according to today's passage.

Archaeologists confirm the Israelite settlement, promised by God, as historical fact. The settlement appears, however, to have been attained in a more piecemeal manner than is described in Joshua. The Hebrew invasion was, historically, less ordered and more chaotic, a process of guerrilla warfare in the forested hill country. The newcomers did not have the 'chariots of iron' mentioned in verse 18, so their military dealings with the Canaanites would have been tricky, to say the least. They found space for themselves not just through the retreat of the then occupants but also through deforestation. The archaeological evidence points to a continuous settlement, which brought with it cultural conflict. For example, there was intermarriage, which is evidence of different faiths coexisting.

However the settlement occurred, suddenly or gradually, the Israelite response to God's gift was demonstrably lacking. Again and again this favoured people, offered a goodly heritage, threw away their chances. The book of Joshua is both the corollary of the book of the Law (Pentateuch) and a curtain-raiser to this chronic failure of Israel to live in gratitude and obedience to the God who had called them.

Lord, we thank you with Israel for your calling to us and the grace to fulfil it. Guide our steps to places and people you have ready for us today. Overshadow our dealings, with peace surpassing human understanding.

JOHN TWISLETON

Tranquillity town

'Provide three men from each tribe, and I will send them out that they may begin to go throughout the land, writing a description of it with a view to their inheritances. Then come back to me...' So the men went and traversed the land and set down in a book a description of it by towns in seven divisions; then they came back to Joshua in the camp at Shiloh, and Joshua cast lots for them in Shiloh before the Lord; and there Joshua apportioned the land to the Israelites, to each a portion.

The Judeo-Christian tradition has both directional and cyclical elements. God's people are on the move with God, and yet, in our worship, we follow cycles linked to natural and church seasons. There are also holy places that we come back to, as part of our forward journey of faith.

Shiloh was such a place, before Jerusalem became 'the' place. Long before Joshua and the Israelites arrived there, back in the Bronze Age, Shiloh was a walled city with a shrine. Just as, in later centuries, Christian evangelisation maintained yet transformed sites of pagan worship, so the Israelites set up their tent for meeting the living God in a place seen as holy in previous generations.

One translation of Shiloh is 'Tranquillity town', which catches something of its instrumentality within the Israelite settlement described here. By casting lots, Joshua apportioned land and security to his assembled congregation. As we read on to chapter 22:1–34, however, matters seem less tranquil, with Israelite tribes appearing to set up a rival shrine by the Jordan, which Phinehas is sent to sort out.

We come from God; we belong to God; we go to God. The Joshua story is a powerful reminder that faith is a journey with clear direction. The nurturing of any faith community also requires a cycle of worship in which holy places and pilgrimage destinations play their part alongside devotions that are seasonal and repetitive.

As the church's Easter season nears completion, let us thank God for its reminder of the exodus completed for us in Christ's victory over death, and our own promised land of heaven.

JOHN TWISLETON

Working out salvation

When they had finished distributing the several territories of the land as inheritances, the Israelites gave an inheritance among them to Joshua son of Nun. By command of the Lord they gave him the town that he asked for, Timnath-serah in the hill country of Ephraim; he rebuilt the town, and settled in it.

We come to the conclusion of the distribution of land, with Joshua him-self, last but not least. Notice the weaving together of two oral traditions in the settlement narrative, which have either Joshua or the Israelites allocating the land. In verse 50 we are reminded, especially in Joshua's own case, that the real allocator is the Lord, even though he gives Joshua what he wants.

As the passage makes clear, this gift, like most gifts we receive from God, implies a task—in this case, the rebuilding of the town. Our personal history as believers is just such a combination, as we read in Paul's letter to Philippi: 'Work out your own salvation with fear and trembling; for it is God who is at work in you, enabling you both to will and to work for his good pleasure' (Philippians 2:12b–13). That work, like Joshua's, is God's gift to be unwrapped and worked out. The collaboration of grace with faithful action is rather like building a concrete path. We make a remova-ble wooden frame and pour in the cement so that, though we put work in, only the concrete endures once it's set.

Jewish tradition places the tombs of both Caleb and Joshua in Timnath-serah, meaning a 'portion of abundance'. In Judges 2:9, Joshua's town is called by the slightly different name of Timnath-here, meaning 'portion of the sun'. The difference picks up on the miraculous holding of the sun in the sky at Joshua's behest in Joshua 10:13. However we see this miracle, we cannot deny the lofty expectations throughout the book of Joshua, immortalised in the title of his burial place.

How many of my tasks today will be a working out of God's promises to me and through me? Is there a need to reschedule my day?

JOHN TWISLETON

Finding sanctuary

Then the Lord spoke to Joshua, saying, 'Say to the Israelites, "Appoint the cities of refuge, of which I spoke to you through Moses, so that anyone who kills a person without intent or by mistake may flee there; they shall be for you a refuge from the avenger of blood. The slayer shall flee to one of these cities and shall stand at the entrance of the gate of the city, and explain the case to the elders of that city; then the fugitive shall be taken into the city, and given a place, and shall remain with them."'

The church I serve—St Giles, Horsted Keynes in West Sussex—has a particularly warm ambience, a feeling of welcome that many remark upon in the visitors' book. It has stood for almost 1000 years, and some believe that its welcoming feel is linked to its being assigned in the Middle Ages as a sanctuary church, one of several in Chichester Diocese set apart for fugitives seeking justice. If they escaped the pursuing lynch mob into St Giles and on to the sanctuary stool, fugitives were guaranteed due process of law.

Such traditions mirror the one recorded in this passage, which provides a detail of Israel's settlement in the appointing of cities of refuge 'so that anyone who kills a person without intent or by mistake may flee there; they shall be for you a refuge from the avenger of blood' (v. 3). God wants it to be recognised that the severity of any wrongdoing is linked to the intention of the accused. This is key to his working out of his love for Israel into structures that serve social justice.

Retribution is an important part of the justice system across the world, flowing from Judeo-Christian ethics. It is to be tempered by mercy, of which Joshua's cities of refuge and the sanctuary stools of medieval Christendom are an illustration. Joshua's God may seem at times so holy as to utterly reject transgressors but he also loves his people and provides for their frailty.

God treats me as better than I am. How do I treat others?

JOHN TWISLETON

Unfailing promises

Thus the Lord gave to Israel all the land that he swore to their ancestors that he would give them; and having taken possession of it, they settled there. And the Lord gave them rest on every side just as he had sworn to their ancestors; not one of all their enemies had withstood them, for the Lord had given all their enemies into their hands. Not one of all the good promises that the Lord had made to the house of Israel had failed; all came to pass.

One of the great benefits of reading the Bible is that we develop a growing familiarity with the promises of God and how they find sure delivery when they are acted upon. Reading the biblical story of Israel brings insight into God's faithfulness over the call of a nation with a special purpose. God's call and the promise of land are fulfilled in the settlement executed by Joshua. 'Not one of all the good promises that the Lord had made to the house of Israel had failed; all came to pass' (v. 45).

A key part of biblical literacy is a familiarisation with the promises of God both for the believing community and for individual believers. In my own experience, promise verses that have blessed me and that I've committed to memory come regularly into play. They include 'My peace I give to you' (John 14:27) and 'In returning and rest you shall be saved; in quietness and in trust shall be your strength' (Isaiah 30:15).

The tumult of our lives is stilled by repeating God's promises. There is no word of God without power, but without knowing God's word and the passages he has blessed to us individually, we are at a total disadvantage—we have no promises to lay hold of when we're in serious need. I have mentioned passages that especially breathe God's peace and put me at rest, since this passage indicates that the fulfilment of God's promises to Israel under Joshua was that he 'gave them rest on every side' (v. 44).

'The Lord gave them rest on every side.' Does this verse have a bearing for me? Is there a decision or task I need to accomplish, to enter godly rest?

JOHN TWISLETON

Moral demands come second

Then Joshua summoned the Reubenites, the Gadites, and the half-tribe of Manasseh, and said to them, '... Take good care to observe the commandment and instruction that Moses the servant of the Lord commanded you, to love the Lord your God, to walk in all his ways, to keep his commandments, and to hold fast to him, and to serve him with all your heart and with all your soul.' So Joshua blessed them and sent them away, and they went to their tents.

One great distortion of Christianity today is the perception that it's a 'super morality'—and people are prevented from seeing this distortion for what it is by imprudent Christian commentators on morality, who are easy game for a public that is increasingly unsympathetic to the claims of revealed faith.

Joshua's invitation to love God and keep his commandments, like that of his predecessor Moses, is set within a context of gratitude for God's love for his people. That love was shown to Israel by her miraculous delivery from slavery in Egypt and the settlement in Canaan, which the books of Exodus and Joshua record. The Christian ethic has a similar context: 'We love because he first loved us' (1 John 4:19). God's love is shown to us in our passing through the waters of baptism, to shake off our slavery to sin and enter the promised country of grace in company with the Church of Jesus Christ.

Only as we regularly count our blessings do we recognise ourselves as folk on the move, as surely as the people of God under Joshua's leadership were on the move. That grateful sense is a pointer to a religion of high moral calling, yes, but one that is chiefly pervaded by the mercy of God, for whose call we have no rational explanation.

The Joshua story is a typical biblical pointer to a God of grace whose moral demands are second to his love and purpose for those he calls—those who readily 'hold fast to him, and serve him with all their heart and with all their soul' (v. 5).

Gracious Lord, help me so to love you that I infect others with that love, which is itself your gift. Amen

JOHN TWISLETON

Rest in the Lord

A long time afterwards, when the Lord had given rest to Israel from all their enemies all around, and Joshua was old and well advanced in years, Joshua summoned all Israel, their elders and heads, their judges and officers, and said to them, 'I am now old and well advanced in years; and you have seen all that the Lord your God has done to all these nations for your sake, for it is the Lord your God who has fought for you... Therefore be very steadfast to observe and do all that is written in the book of the law of Moses, turning aside from it neither to the right nor to the left.'

I remember a bishop making something of a backhanded compliment to a colleague: 'There's no sabbath rest for the people of God in Father Smith's parish!' He was picking up on the proactive leadership style of that priest, but with evident sympathy for his people!

Both Joshua and Hebrews speak of a sabbath rest for God's people. We read in verse 1 how, in Joshua's old age, 'the Lord had given rest to Israel from all their enemies all around', and this sets the scene for Joshua's farewell address. It also sets the scene for a reflection, 1300 years later, by the author of Hebrews on the promised land in the age to come: 'For if Joshua had given them rest, God would not speak later about another day. So then, a sabbath rest still remains for the people of God' (Hebrews 4:8–9).

The temporary rest attained by Joshua in the settlement is seen, later in scripture, to foreshadow the eternal rest and peace of the Christian departed. 'Eternal rest grant unto them, O Lord,' we pray at funerals, 'and let light perpetual shine upon them.'

The rest of the eternal sabbath of heaven has traditionally been anticipated in the peace of both Jewish and Christian sabbaths, which is now so eroded by commerce across the world. To come back to 'Father Smith', the activism of many churches can also be counter to the sacred truth of Sunday rest.

'Rest in the Lord, and wait patiently for him' (Psalm 37:7, KJV).

JOHN TWISLETON

All-consuming holiness

Then the people answered, 'Far be it from us that we should forsake the Lord to serve other gods; for it is the Lord our God who brought us and our ancestors up from the land of Egypt, out of the house of slavery…' But Joshua said to the people, 'You cannot serve the Lord, for he is a holy God. He is a jealous God; he will not forgive your transgressions or your sins. If you forsake the Lord and serve foreign gods, then he will turn and do you harm, and consume you, after having done you good.' And the people said to Joshua, 'No, we will serve the Lord!'

A lot of biblical research has gone into Joshua 24, which links to covenant ceremonies outside Judaism and to the previous covenants with Abraham and Moses. The various biblical covenants between God and his people have both conditional and unconditional elements.

What is the nature of covenant in the book of Joshua? It links to the vision of God given to Moses at Sinai, one of holiness requiring obedience; hence, it is mostly conditional. God is seen to bless and yet to curse: 'He is a jealous God; he will not forgive your transgressions or your sins' (v. 19). Yet in this concluding narrative of Joshua we see both judgement and mercy in God's welcome of his people as they confess their unfaithfulness and profess, 'We will serve the Lord' (v. 21).

The idea of a loving God purging his people with fire survives into the New Testament and Christian devotion. The letter to the Hebrews says, 'Let us give thanks, by which we offer to God an acceptable worship with reverence and awe; for indeed our God is a consuming fire' (Hebrews 12:28–29).

Thankfulness and awe before God are evident in the people's dialogue with Joshua, recalling the mighty work of the exodus. It is at the heart of the Christian Eucharist (Greek for 'thanksgiving'). Forgetfulness of God leads to presumption. Such pride undermines our relationship with him, so we should ask him to burn it away and make us aflame with holiness.

Lord, consume in me all that is unworthy of you. Come, Holy Spirit, and kindle your flame within me.

JOHN TWISLETON

Ascension day

Clap your hands, all you peoples; shout to God with loud songs of joy. For the Lord, the Most High, is awesome, a great king over all the earth… God has gone up with a shout, the Lord with the sound of a trumpet. Sing praises to God, sing praises; sing praises to our King, sing praises. For God is the king of all the earth; sing praises with a psalm.

We break from our daily reflections on Joshua to mark the major Christian festival of the ascension of our Lord Jesus Christ. The liturgy of the day includes Psalm 47, and a number of churches will use William Croft's setting of verse 5 in Tudor English, 'God has gone up with a merry noise' as festal music.

Festal singing, shouting, clapping and trumpeting are associated with the enthronement of the kings of Israel, which seems to have been the pretext for affirming God's own kingship over all. As the kings took their seats, the people, led by the choir, gave praise to God as supreme ruler.

Much of our Christian liturgy is built from the Psalms, so it is no surprise to see Psalm 47 used to mark and engage with Christ's ascension and enthronement as universal King. God's sovereignty is now exercised through his Son, 'who ascended into heaven, is seated at the right hand of the Father, and will come to judge the living and the dead' (Apostles' Creed).

Jesus is Lord! He has 'gone up with a merry noise'. The carpenter born in Nazareth who shows the world the love, truth and power of God—he is Lord! A life of 33 years, lived at the start of our era, continues the same yesterday, today and for ever 'through the power of an indestructible life' (Hebrews 7:16b). Jesus is Lord above all that is or has been or will be. He is God's final word to humankind. Jesus is to be the merciful last word over us all.

'Sing praises to God, sing praises; sing praises to our King, sing praises. For God is the king of all the earth; sing praises with a psalm' (Psalm 47:6–7).

JOHN TWISLETON

Sacramental gifts

The people said to Joshua, 'The Lord our God we will serve, and him we will obey.' So Joshua made a covenant with the people that day, and made statutes and ordinances for them at Shechem. Joshua wrote these words in the book of the law of God; and he took a large stone, and set it up there under the oak in the sanctuary of the Lord... So Joshua sent the people away to their inheritances.

The narrative of Joshua's covenant-making concludes with the erection of the Shechem stone as a sign of the people's decision for God.

The Bible has a sacramental vision of the material world, showing it again and again as God's instrument. A related passage to this is in Genesis 28:11–12, where we read of Jacob's dream inspired by a stone: '[Jacob] came to a certain place and stayed there for the night, because the sun had set. Taking one of the stones of the place, he put it under his head and lay down in that place. And he dreamed that there was a ladder set up on the earth, the top of it reaching to heaven; and the angels of God were ascending and descending on it.'

Since the ladder image and the image of sacrificed animals are Old Testament pointers to Jesus Christ, we might leap forward to ponder the new covenant sealed in his blood. Like Joshua's sacred stone, the sacred meal of the Eucharist is a pointer to that new and everlasting covenant, not just calling God's Son to mind but calling him into our midst. 'For as often as you eat this bread and drink the cup, you proclaim [show] the Lord's death until he comes' (1 Corinthians 11:26).

There is a pointer in Joshua 24:24–26 to the power of sacraments to manifest the word of God. Baptism, Eucharist, confession, anointing, confirmation, marriage and ordination are all outward signs of new covenant gifts.

Do we see these love gifts in relation to that covenant, and do we welcome grace through their physical impact? God invisible is making his love visible, engaging with our make-up, body and soul.

JOHN TWISLETON

God is salvation

After these things Joshua son of Nun, the servant of the Lord, died, being one hundred and ten years old. They buried him in his own inheritance at Timnath-serah, which is in the hill country of Ephraim, north of Mount Gaash. Israel served the Lord all the days of Joshua, and all the days of the elders who outlived Joshua and had known all the work that the Lord did for Israel. The bones of Joseph, which the Israelites had brought up from Egypt, were buried at Shechem, in the portion of ground that Jacob had bought from the children of Hamor.

Joseph, Joshua and Jesus fit together. Joseph takes Israel into Egypt, saving them from starvation. Joshua finishes the task of taking Israel out of Egypt and physical servitude. Jesus leads Israel out of the servitude of sin into 'the freedom of the glory of the children of God (Romans 8:21).

Joshua dies, like Joseph, at 110 years. The burial of the two leaders coincides and marks the end of the exodus and settlement. Their burial in this land is proof that God has fulfilled his promise, since the land is now Israel's. As Joseph enters Egypt through suffering and rises to political power, Jesus enters glory through suffering. Joshua has less suffering but his name, like 'Jesus' in Greek, means 'God is salvation'. The writer of Hebrews compares the period of rest in Canaan that Joshua won for Israel to the eternal rest promised to the new Israel, which is the Church of Jesus Christ (Hebrews 4:8–9).

Joshua's burial place of Timnath-serah, meaning a 'portion of abundance' (or, in Judges 2:9, Tinmath-heres, 'portion of the sun') reminds us of his miracles. The last place of Jesus has not been seen, for his mortal end coincided with the end of mortality, and he is 'the same yesterday and today and for ever' (Hebrews 13:8).

'God is salvation' through Joseph, Joshua and Jesus. We can't read of one without engaging with the others, and chiefly the new Joshua, Jesus Christ. His readiness to save is here and now for the sick and sinful, sorrowful and dying, lost and distracted.

Jesus, new Joshua, may your saving love embrace us.
Bring us through this vale of tears to rejoice in your heavenly country.

JOHN TWISLETON

35

The Holy Spirit

The Holy Spirit offers a rich seam of exploration for our next series of reflections. I have chosen to pass over some of the most familiar passages, such as Acts 2:1–13 and 1 Corinthians 12:8–10, in favour of a broad sweep of references moving sequentially (more or less) through the whole Bible.

We first read of the work of the Spirit in the first creation account in Genesis, where 'a wind from God' sweeps over the face of the waters (Genesis 1:2). Next, the Spirit is manifested in the creative gifts of individual craftsmen working on the construction of the tabernacle (Exodus 35:30–34), and in the recognition of the need for individual repentance (Psalm 51:6–12). The Spirit is concerned, in Isaiah 32:14–18, with the renewal of the land and, in Ezekiel 37:1–11, the renewal of the nation and its people.

With these last two prophecies we are standing on the edge of a new threshold, and with the prophecy of Joel 2:28–29 ('I will pour out my spirit on all flesh…') we are propelled beyond it. No more will the Spirit be given only to specific people for particular tasks; in the future, the Spirit is to be bestowed universally, with a lavish, reckless prodigality. Jesus echoes this lavishness when he refers to the Spirit as 'living water' that will flow from the believer's heart (John 7:38), and when he breathes the Spirit into his terrified disciples, bringing peace and joy (John 20:22).

The descent of the Spirit on Jesus at his baptism comes with words of assurance and affirmation, but as Jesus is then immediately 'driven out' by the Spirit into the wilderness to be tempted, we are reminded that we may expect the Spirit's presence in our lives to be deeply challenging. With Nicodemus, in John 3, we struggle to grasp something of the workings of the Spirit, and with the apostles we thrill at the promise of the coming Spirit's power (Acts 1:8). After two examples of Paul's wisdom on the nitty-gritty realities of daily life and relationships in the Spirit, from Galatians 5 and 1 Corinthians 13, our final reflection, from Revelation 22, revisits the 'living water' metaphor and issues an invitation and welcome to all: 'Come.'

BARBARA MOSSE

A wind from God

In the beginning when God created the heavens and the earth, the earth was a formless void and darkness covered the face of the deep, while a wind from God swept over the face of the waters. Then God said, 'Let there be light'; and there was light. And God saw that the light was good; and God separated the light from the darkness. God called the light Day, and the darkness he called Night. And there was evening and there was morning, the first day... God saw everything that he had made, and indeed, it was very good.

How is it possible for human beings even to begin to articulate the wonder and mystery that is God? The book of Genesis makes a courageous and graphic attempt by looking back to the very beginning of all things, picturing the creative forces of God interacting with the 'formless void and darkness' of pre-creation chaos. The original Hebrew term for 'wind' (*ruach*) is much richer in meaning than the English translation, encompassing also the idea of 'breath' and 'spirit'. These strands of meaning are picked up in other biblical translations, and all of them help to make the presence and involvement of God's Spirit in the work of creation explicit.

This is tremendously good news, because the text implies that even back in the earliest dawn of prehistory, God entered into relationship with his creation. In his novel *The Magician's Nephew*, C.S. Lewis memorably describes the creation of Narnia by picturing the lion Aslan singing the creation into being. And for the priest-poet Gerard Manley Hopkins, in his wonderful poem 'God's grandeur', the relationship between God's Spirit and his creation is maternal and nurturing:

> *Oh, morning, at the brown brink eastwards, springs—*
> *Because the Holy Ghost over the bent*
> *World broods with warm breast and with ah! bright wings.*

'Oh Lord... the earth is full of your creatures... When you send forth your spirit, they are created; and you renew the face of the ground' (Psalm 104:24, 30). In what ways do you experience the Holy Spirit nurturing your life and creativity?

BARBARA MOSSE

Beauty and skill

Then Moses said to the Israelites: See, the Lord has called by name Bezalel son of Uri son of Hur, of the tribe of Judah; he has filled him with divine spirit, with skill, intelligence, and knowledge in every kind of craft, to devise artistic designs, to work in gold, silver, and bronze, in cutting stones for setting, and in carving wood, in every kind of craft. And he has inspired him to teach, both him and Oholiab son of Ahisamach, of the tribe of Dan. He has filled them with skill to do every kind of work... by any sort of artisan or skilled designer.

These final chapters in the book of Exodus are all concerned with the pressing need to provide an earthly home for the holy. Previous chapters have described Moses' encounter with God on Mt Sinai and his return with the two 'tablets of the covenant' (34:29). A sanctuary is now to be built to house them, and despite the holiness of the task there is a refreshing, down-to-earth approach to the project's practicalities. The tasks may be practical but they are to be imbued with 'divine spirit, with skill, intelligence, and knowledge in every kind of craft' (35:31). This work is to be inbreathed by the very Spirit of God.

I sense a parallel here with the days of the early church, when the number of new believers grew to such an extent that the apostles appointed others to take on the practical tasks (Acts 6:1–4). Both accounts, from Exodus and Acts, carry a strong sense of calling, and in both the presence of the Spirit is vital. Like Bezalel and Oholiab, the men chosen in Acts 6 are also to be 'of good standing, full of the Spirit and of wisdom' (6:3). Practical tasks—both then and now—are as spiritually vital as the apostles' prayer and preaching.

All may of thee partake; nothing can be so mean
which, with this tincture—'For thy sake'—will not grow bright and clean.

A servant with this clause makes drudgery divine;
who sweeps a room as for thy laws makes that and the action fine.
                                    'The Elixir', George Herbert (1593–1633)
                                                    BARBARA MOSSE

A clean heart

You desire truth in the inward being; therefore teach me wisdom in my secret heart. Purge me with hyssop, and I shall be clean; wash me, and I shall be whiter than snow. Let me hear joy and gladness; let the bones that you have crushed rejoice. Hide your face from my sins, and blot out all my iniquities. Create in me a clean heart, O God, and put a new and right spirit within me. Do not cast me away from your presence, and do not take your holy spirit from me. Restore to me the joy of your salvation, and sustain in me a willing spirit.

Today's reading from Psalm 51, traditionally one of the psalms of David, focuses our attention on sin, a wearyingly stubborn feature of our human experience. The church adopted this as one of the seven 'penitential psalms' (see also Psalms 6; 32; 38; 102; 130; 143), and although it finds a particular focus in the liturgical calendar on Ash Wednesday, its message is always significant. As A. Whitney Brown once wrote about human history, 'Any good history book is mainly just a long list of mistakes, complete with names and dates. It's very embarrassing' (*The Big Picture: An American Commentary*).

Embarrassing indeed, and the psalm's author has clearly experienced a strong conviction of his own sin before God. He owns his lack of wisdom, his need for forgiveness and for a clean heart. He pleads that God will not drive him from his presence, or take the Holy Spirit away from him. He recognises that only the presence of God's Spirit can restore him and enable him to stay on the right path.

But (thankfully!) this psalm isn't just about human sin; it is preeminently about the loving nature of God and his endless willingness to forgive and recreate. This is indeed good news, but it requires our willingness to be honest with God and aware of our constant need for him.

How do we face the reality of our own sin? How do we accept its inevitability without becoming complacent or indifferent?
Can we stand openly before God, trusting in the power of his Spirit to forgive, cleanse and renew?

BARBARA MOSSE

Quietness and trust

For the palace will be forsaken, the populous city deserted; the hill and the watch-tower will become dens for ever, the joy of wild asses, a pasture for flocks; until a spirit from on high is poured out upon us, and the wilderness becomes a fruitful field, and the fruitful field is deemed a forest. Then justice will dwell in the wilderness, and righteousness abide in the fruitful field. The effect of righteousness will be peace, and the result of righteousness, quietness and trust for ever. My people will abide in a peaceful habitation, in secure dwellings, and in quiet resting-places.

Scholars have found it difficult to date this passage, some placing it as early as the time of Josiah in the seventh century BC, while others tend more towards the exilic or post-exilic periods. It is part of a longer narrative, of course (32:1–20), in which verse 14 brings to an end a series of warnings and predictions of future disaster. Then comes a picture of harmony and fruitfulness in the natural world, and righteousness, justice and peace among its inhabitants (vv. 15–18).

The hinge between the warnings and the promise lies in verse 15: '… until a spirit from on high is poured out on us, and the wilderness becomes a fruitful field'. The 'spirit from on high' is to be the agent of healing, but the initial focus of that transformation is to be the land rather than its inhabitants. The healing of the land will enable God's people to live with justice in 'a peaceful habitation, in secure dwellings, and in quiet resting-places' (v. 18).

With today's frenetic pace of life and with a continuing tension between overdevelopment of the land on one hand and the desperate need for more homes on the other, it may seem to us that 'quiet resting-places' are increasingly hard to find. Perhaps a passage such as this one challenges us to look again at our own sense of rootedness—or lack of it—and of the need for all of us to seek the ultimate sense of belonging that we can find only in God.

*'In returning and rest you shall be saved; in quietness
and in trust shall be your strength' (Isaiah 30:15).*

BARBARA MOSSE

Can these bones live?

The hand of the Lord came upon me, and he brought me out by the spirit of the Lord and set me down in the middle of a valley; it was full of bones. He led me all round them; there were very many lying in the valley, and they were very dry. He said to me, 'Mortal, can these bones live?' I answered, 'O Lord God, you know.' Then he said to me, 'Prophesy to these bones, and say to them, O dry bones, hear the word of the Lord. Thus says the Lord God to these bones: I will cause breath to enter you, and you shall live. I will lay sinews upon you, and will cause flesh to come upon you, and cover you with skin, and put breath in you, and you shall live; and you shall know that I am the Lord.'…I prophesied as he commanded me, and the breath came into them, and they lived, and stood upon their feet, a vast multitude. Then he said to me, 'Mortal, these bones are the whole house of Israel.'

The prophet's vision of the valley of dry bones is arguably the most famous passage in Ezekiel. This passage describes the third of four reported visions (the others are in 1:1–3, 15; 8:1—11:25; and 40:1—48:35). Each vision is accompanied by Ezekiel's statement: 'The hand of the Lord came upon me.' In today's passage, the Spirit of the Lord is experienced in two ways: as a means of transporting the prophet from one place to another (v. 1), and in literally 'inspiring' the dry bones and bringing them back to life (vv. 5–6). As shown in verse 11, Ezekiel's message was originally directed at the nation of Israel as a whole, but it works equally well on an individual level. We may experience times of dryness and a loss of hope, but if God is able to restore desiccated bones and bring buried bodies back to life, then there are no limits to his power in your life or in mine.

'Jesus answered, "Very truly, I tell you, no one can enter the kingdom of God without being born of water and Spirit. What is born of the flesh is flesh, and what is born of the Spirit is spirit"' (John 3:5–6).

BARBARA MOSSE

On all flesh

I will repay you for the years that the swarming locust has eaten... You shall eat in plenty and be satisfied, and praise the name of the Lord your God, who has dealt wondrously with you. And my people shall never again be put to shame... Then afterwards I will pour out my spirit on all flesh; your sons and your daughters shall prophesy, your old men shall dream dreams, and your young men shall see visions. Even on the male and female slaves, in those days, I will pour out my spirit... The sun shall be turned to darkness, and the moon to blood, before the great and terrible day of the Lord comes. Then everyone who calls on the name of the Lord shall be saved.

This well-known prophecy of Joel is one of a group of biblical writings that come under the heading of 'apocalyptic'—prophecies that deal with the action of God in the world at the end of time. Blood, darkness, fire and smoke are the symbols of the apocalypse that the author uses here (vv. 30–31), preceding the judgement that will come with 'the great and terrible day of the Lord'.

This apocalyptic prophecy is not just about the end times, however; it also had an immediate application for the people who first heard it. The date of the book's writing is unclear but the national problems being faced by the nation are not: the country had come under enemy attack (Joel 1:6–7), and, as a 'double whammy', had suffered a devastating plague of locusts (Joel 1:4).

There is something deeply moving about God's promise to repay Israel 'for the years that the swarming locust has eaten' (2:25); the promised restoration (vv. 26–27) will be followed by a universal gift of God's Spirit (vv. 28–29). There is a lavish abundance in the language used here, foreshadowing similar extravagant outpourings of God's love in the New Testament (Luke 6:38; Matthew 14:13–21).

'The wind blows where it chooses, and you hear the sound of it,
but you do not know where it comes from or where it goes.
So it is with everyone who is born of the Spirit' (John 3:8).

BARBARA MOSSE

Rivers of living water

On the last day of the festival, the great day, while Jesus was standing there, he cried out, 'Let anyone who is thirsty come to me, and let the one who believes in me drink. As the scripture has said, "Out of the believer's heart shall flow rivers of living water."' Now he said this about the Spirit, which believers in him were to receive; for as yet there was no Spirit, because Jesus was not yet glorified.

The image Jesus uses in this passage—living water—is a familiar one. John picks up a clear link with his earlier account of Jesus' meeting with the Samaritan woman at Jacob's well (John 4:1–42). There, Jesus used the presence of literal water as a bridge to the living water that he will give: 'a spring of water gushing up to eternal life'. In today's passage, this living water is directly linked to the promised gift of the Holy Spirit (v. 39).

John's comment that 'as yet there was no Spirit' may seem puzzling at first; haven't we in these reflections seen examples of the earlier working of God's Spirit, even in the Old Testament? But it is important to remember that John is writing out of a particular understanding of the church, which did not exist before the resurrection. It was Jesus' death, resurrection and ascension that cast the whole work of the Holy Spirit into a completely new light.

There is another puzzle, too. We may have expected Jesus to follow his invitation ('Let anyone who is thirsty come to me', vv. 37–38) with words like '… and you won't be thirsty again'. But what he actually says is somewhat different (v. 38). His meaning seems to be, 'Come to me and drink, and then *you* will be able to relieve the thirst of others.' Surely, this can offer positive hope when we consider all those apparently impossible demands of Jesus: 'Love your enemies and pray for those who persecute you' (Matthew 5:44), or 'deny yourselves and take up your cross' (see Luke 9:23). Drink from this fountain of living water, Christ seems to be saying, and even the impossible becomes possible.

Forgive us our sins, as we forgive those who sin against us.

BARBARA MOSSE

Receive the Holy Spirit

When it was evening on that day, the first day of the week, and the doors of the house where the disciples had met were locked for fear of the Jews, Jesus came and stood among them and said, 'Peace be with you.' After he said this, he showed them his hands and his side. Then the disciples rejoiced when they saw the Lord. Jesus said to them again, 'Peace be with you. As the Father has sent me, so I send you.' When he had said this, he breathed on them and said, 'Receive the Holy Spirit. If you forgive the sins of any, they are forgiven them; if you retain the sins of any, they are retained.'

Acts 2:1–13 describes the coming of the Holy Spirit in a dramatic and very public way; our passage today from John's Gospel offers us a quieter and more private counterpart. With this event, taking place during one of Christ's resurrection appearances to his disciples, the distance between Easter and Pentecost collapses (Gail R. O'Day, *New Interpreter's Bible*, p. 848). In John's understanding, the empowering of the disciples with the Spirit signifies both the Easter message (resurrection) and the beginning of the infant church's mission: the two cannot be separated. Jesus breathes the Spirit on them, conveying his peace and the commission to minister in his name and continue his work in the world.

The words about forgiving and retaining sins are difficult, but John's particular understanding of sin is important here. Elsewhere in this Gospel, John describes sin as being a blindness to the revelation of God in Jesus Christ (John 9:41). Sin, for John, is a refusal to see the truth of that revelation, rather than simply bad behaviour or questionable morals (compare Matthew 18:18). When the Gospel states that part of the Spirit's role is to 'prove the world wrong about sin' (John 16:8), it points to a revelation of the limitless love of the Father for his creation, and the possibility for the world to choose, through Christ, to enter into that relationship of love.

Breathe on me, breath of God; fill me with life anew,
that I may love what thou dost love, and do what thou wouldst do.

Edwin Hatch (1835–89)

BARBARA MOSSE

Driven out

In those days Jesus came from Nazareth of Galilee and was baptized by John in the Jordan. And just as he was coming up out of the water, he saw the heavens torn apart and the Spirit descending like a dove on him. And a voice came from heaven, 'You are my Son, the beloved; with you I am well pleased.' And the Spirit immediately drove him out into the wilderness. He was in the wilderness for forty days, tempted by Satan; and he was with the wild beasts; and the angels waited on him.

There is a wonderful scene in that historic artistic masterpiece the Bayeux Tapestry, which shows King Harold urging his troops into battle by prodding them from behind with a spear. The accompanying description states, 'King Harold comforteth his troops.' This is something of a shock to us, who are used to the term 'comfort' indicating physical ease or relief from pain or discomfort. But the word's origins are very different, coming from the Latin *com* (expressing intensive force) and *fortis* (strong). When Jesus foretells the coming of the Holy Spirit as the Comforter in John 14:26 (KJV), it is this earlier meaning of robust strength that it carries.

In today's reading, we see the Spirit at work in two ways. Initially the Spirit descends on Jesus 'like a dove' at his baptism, accompanying words of reassurance that Jesus is indeed God's Son. But then immediately, states Mark, the Spirit *drove* Jesus out into the wilderness for 40 days to be tempted by Satan. Mark's 'drove' (literally, to 'throw out') is far nearer to the original sense of the Spirit as Comforter than is the more genteel 'led' that we find in Luke 4:1 and Matthew 4:1. It implies a sense of urgency and insistent intent on the part of the Spirit, and, arguably, an element of natural human resistance on the part of Jesus. When we pray for the Spirit to fill our hearts and lives, how do we expect it to happen?

O Comforter, draw near, within my heart appear,
and kindle it, thy holy flame bestowing.

O let it freely burn, till earthly passions turn
to dust and ashes in its heat consuming.

'Come down, O Love divine', Bianco da Siena (d. 1434)

BARBARA MOSSE

Born from above

Jesus answered [Nicodemus], 'Very truly, I tell you, no one can enter the kingdom of God without being born of water and Spirit. What is born of the flesh is flesh, and what is born of the Spirit is spirit… The wind blows where it chooses, and you hear the sound of it, but you do not know where it comes from or where it goes. So it is with everyone who is born of the Spirit.' Nicodemus said to him, 'How can these things be?' Jesus answered him, 'Are you a teacher of Israel, and yet you do not understand these things?'

Nicodemus was a Pharisee and a leader of the Jews, who famously visited Jesus 'by night' (3:2). There was a real risk here for Nicodemus; as a leader of the Sanhedrin, to approach such a controversial figure as Jesus openly and with such genuine interest would have exposed him to the suspicion and censure of his colleagues, if nothing worse. Nicodemus is puzzled: how can it be possible for a person to be born again (3:4)? When Jesus' explanation does nothing to disperse his mental fog, Jesus chides him: 'Are you a teacher of Israel, and yet you do not understand these things?' (v. 10).

Jesus seems to be saying that although the Spirit has not yet been widely given, the signs are there, and have been for generations of Israel's history. As one of the religious leaders in Israel, Nicodemus was in the perfect position to have picked up those signs. Instead, he has become trapped in a literal interpretation of Jesus' words. In describing the totally new thing that is happening, Jesus returns to the wind/spirit imagery of the first Genesis creation account, an association that must surely have resonated with Nicodemus. In our familiarity with the Gospel story, are there vital signs that we too miss about the new thing the Spirit is seeking to work in our lives?

*'Do not remember the former things, or consider the things of old.
I am about to do a new thing; now it springs forth, do you not perceive it?
I will make a way in the wilderness and rivers in the desert…
to give drink to my chosen people' (Isaiah 43:18–20, abridged).*

BARBARA MOSSE

You will receive power

[The apostles] asked him, 'Lord, is this the time when you will restore the kingdom to Israel?' He replied, 'It is not for you to know the times or the periods that the Father has set... But you will receive power when the Holy Spirit has come upon you; and you will be my witnesses in Jerusalem, in all Judea and Samaria, and to the ends of the earth.' When he had said this, as they were watching, he was lifted up, and a cloud took him out of their sight... Then they returned to Jerusalem... [and] went to the room upstairs where they were staying... constantly devoting themselves to prayer, together with certain women, including Mary the mother of Jesus, as well as his brothers.

The urgent question in the early chapters of Acts concerns the discipleship of Jesus' followers, and whether they will be capable of continuing the work in his name when they can neither see nor hear him. It is a question that Jesus has been aware of for some time. In John's Gospel, Jesus speaks of the coming Spirit's role in teaching and in reminding the disciples of everything that he himself had said and done (John 14:26). But here in Acts 1, the main emphasis laid on the Spirit's work is in the empowering of the disciples for the ongoing work of mission (v. 8).

Since its very earliest days, the church has wrestled with the relationship between prayer and activity in the work of mission, and the need to find a healthy balance between them. In our churches, what place does the Spirit have in our own thinking? In recent decades, there has been a tendency to see the Spirit as vibrantly present in visible charismatic experience, such as we see in today's passage; less so, perhaps, in those activities inspired in a quieter way by the gentle inbreathing of the Spirit as described in John 20 (see 4 June). Yet both are clearly important, as both point us towards the limitless ways in which God's Holy Spirit moves and works among us.

In what ways does your church recognise the work of the Spirit,
both within its own worshipping life and in the wider community?

BARBARA MOSSE

Live by the Spirit

For freedom Christ has set us free. Stand firm, therefore, and do not submit again to a yoke of slavery... Live by the Spirit, I say, and do not gratify the desires of the flesh. For what the flesh desires is opposed to the Spirit, and what the Spirit desires is opposed to the flesh; for these are opposed to each other, to prevent you from doing what you want... Now the works of the flesh are obvious: fornication, impurity, licentiousness... enmities, strife, jealousy, anger, quarrels, dissensions, factions, envy... By contrast, the fruit of the Spirit is love, joy, peace, patience, kindness, generosity, faithfulness, gentleness and self-control. There is no law against such things.

In today's reading we are on well-trodden ground, but this passage from Galatians is one of many that run the risk of overfamiliarity. I remember the curate of our local church leading an assembly on this topic at my school many years ago. Although I was deeply impressed by his artistic efforts—he had drawn a many-branched plant covered in brightly coloured fruits representing the fruit of the Spirit—I'm not sure I was any the wiser at the time about the implications of what he was saying for my own life.

There is far more at stake here than simply lists of behaviours we should avoid and emulate, and the key to the whole passage lies in verse 1. It comes down to a question of freedom or slavery. Whom—or what—do we serve? Paul is berating the Galatians for heeding those who would have driven them back into spiritual slavery by insisting that, even though they now followed Christ, they should still be living according to the Law. Paul's response is blunt: 'All who rely on the works of the law are under a curse... But if you are led by the Spirit, you are not subject to the law' (Galatians 3:10; 5:18). Rather than slavishly following a pattern of rules and regulations while ignoring damaging behaviour, the community should be looking to the Spirit to heal, guide and transform its way of life.

Reflect for a few moments on your church fellowship and your own place within it, in relation to what Paul teaches in this passage.

BARBARA MOSSE

Love never ends

If I speak in the tongues of mortals and of angels, but do not have love, I am a noisy gong or a clanging cymbal. And if I have prophetic powers, and understand all mysteries and all knowledge, and if I have all faith, so as to remove mountains, but do not have love, I am nothing… Love never ends. But as for prophecies, they will come to an end; as for tongues, they will cease; as for knowledge, it will come to an end… Now I know only in part; then I will know fully, even as I have been fully known. And now faith, hope and love abide, these three; and the greatest of these is love.

Some years ago, I was stopped in the street by a very distressed member of one of our local churches. She was almost in tears. Her church worships in the charismatic tradition and our conversation took place during the height of the Toronto Blessing (a phenomenon characterised by intense experiences of the gifts of the Spirit). 'It's happening all around us,' she said, 'but it's just not happening for us. What are we doing wrong? Why isn't God blessing us?'

The very natural human tendency displayed here probably strikes a chord of recognition with all of us: we worry about what God doesn't seem to be doing in our lives, which we assume—rightly or wrongly—that he is doing in the lives of others. When this happens, we can become so discouraged that we miss the good things he actually is doing. My charismatic friend had become so hooked on the outer 'fireworks' of the Spirit's activity that she was in danger of overlooking the Spirit's inner work—less spectacular, perhaps, but slower-burning and longer-lasting.

This is the tendency that Paul addresses with the Corinthians. The people have been laying too much stress on the outer gifts of the Spirit—prophecy, tongues and the like—and not nearly enough on the Spirit's longer-lasting fruit. The outer manifestations will fade; only the Spirit's threefold fruit of faith, hope and love will endure; 'and the greatest of these is love' (v. 13).

Does this experience resonate in your own life, either as an individual or in terms of your church fellowship?

BARBARA MOSSE

Come!

'See, I am coming soon; my reward is with me, to repay according to everyone's work. I am the Alpha and the Omega, the first and the last, the beginning and the end...It is I, Jesus, who sent my angel to you with this testimony for the churches. I am the root and the descendant of David, the bright morning star.' The Spirit and the bride say, 'Come.' And let everyone who hears say, 'Come.' And let everyone who is thirsty come. Let anyone who wishes take the water of life as a gift.

The Revelation to John is a strange and mysterious book that has perplexed and fascinated Christians down the centuries in equal measure, yet it continues to exert what the theologian Christopher Rowland calls 'a peculiar authority' (*Feasting on the Word*, ed. David Bartlett and Barbara Brown Taylor). Today's passage comes from the closing chapter of the book and, for some readers, that authority has been taken as indicating the imminent return of Jesus and the ending of our world. Every generation since the ascension of Christ, including our own, has seen excited pronouncements about specific dates—followed by disillusion and disappointment. Won't we ever learn from Jesus' warning (Matthew 25:13)?

In today's text it is the cosmic Christ who is speaking ('I am the Alpha and the Omega...') rather than Jesus of Nazareth, but, despite the apocalyptic language, there is a down-to-earth message here for the Christian community. 'This is a call to ministry, not a ticketed invitation to sit in a stadium and watch a spectacle' (Paul 'Skip' Johnson, in *Feasting on the Word*). Speculation about Christ's return does little but distract Christians from the work that still needs to be accomplished in our broken world.

These words offer, preeminently, an invitation: come to Christ. It is issued jointly by the Spirit and the bride, the new Jerusalem, then picked up and echoed throughout time by all who hear. 'And let everyone who is thirsty come. Let anyone who wishes take the water of life as a gift' (v. 18). These words are strongly reminiscent of the 'rivers of living water' spoken of by Jesus (see 3 June). How will we respond to Christ's invitation today?

'The Spirit of the Lord is upon me, because he has anointed me
to bring good news to the poor' (Luke 4:18a).

BARBARA MOSSE

Royalty

Many of us are fascinated by the idea of royalty. In Britain, we're used to thinking of our history in terms of the different dynasties: Tudor, Stuart, Victorian and so on. Although in reality there has been much change in the line of succession, the monarchy still stands as a central symbol of continuity, symbolising the one life of the nation coursing through an often turbulent history. There seems to be a sense that the Crown represents, embodies and even somehow secures peace and order in a world that often lacks both. This is why a royal baby is not just any baby, why a George or Charlotte is not just another celebrity birth, but a sign of hope. Yet many sense a shadow-side to all this—the monarchy's position at the very top of an unjust class structure, its association with militarism and empire, its dissonant position within a basically democratic system. In these islands, people are seldom indifferent to royalty. For better or worse, it strikes deep chords within us.

The British are not unique. Even that most republican of nations, the United States, not only adores the British monarchy but has done much to recreate a similar mythological aura around its elected presidency. Royalty and kingship seem to be perennial concerns of human beings, not least in the Bible. The scriptures are full of good kings and bad kings (and, indeed, queens). David and Solomon spring to mind, as might Ahab or Jezebel—but scripture is interested in so much more than simply telling their stories. Reflections on royalty become central to what the Bible says not only about how humans are to live together, but about what humans are and what God intends for them. They are there in the first chapter of the Bible when God grants men and women 'dominion' over the created world, and in the last chapter when the saints begin their 'reign' with Jesus. And of course, the central figure of the Christian Bible, Jesus, is one around whom contested notions of kingship swirled. Was he the King? What kind of King? To get into these questions is to get into the very heart of the gospel. These are the issues we'll be exploring over the next two weeks.

PETER WADDELL

Kings and queens of creation

Then God said, 'Let us make humankind in our image, according to our likeness; and let them have dominion over the fish of the sea, and over the birds of the air, and over the cattle, and over all the wild animals of the earth, and over every creeping thing that creeps upon the earth.' So God created humankind in his image, in the image of God he created them; male and female he created them.

To be a human being is to be a king or queen of creation. Ours is a royal calling. That's what it means to be made in the image of God and so to exercise dominion over the rest of the creation.

The word 'dominion' has been a sharply controversial one in recent times. Many ecologists blame it for encouraging the idea that human beings can treat other creatures and the natural world with disdain and contempt, cutting it up, experimenting on it and consuming it purely for our own benefit. Now, they say, we are reaping the whirlwind. Sometimes, to put all this right, it is suggested that we should abandon dominion language and consider ourselves as not really different from or 'above' any other creature.

This is a mistake. For one thing, dominion simply expresses a truth: for better or worse, the capacity of human beings deliberately to affect the whole world is much greater than that of any other creature. It is not the dolphins, amazing though they are, who are poisoning our environment but we theirs. Moreover, it was always a mistake to read 'dominion' as if it meant 'domination'—as if Genesis meant that the world was simply there for us to exercise power over for our own selfish ends. God, after all, is our Lord, our *dominus*. He does not dominate us, exploit us and consume us. Dominion in the image of God means loving, serving, protecting and bringing to fullness of life. That's the job of a king or queen of creation. We rule, to let others flourish.

'You know that among the Gentiles, those whom they recognise as their rulers lord it over them, and their great ones are tyrants over them. But it is not so among you' (Mark 10:42–43).

PETER WADDELL

War of all against all

The Benjaminites did so; they took wives for each of them from the dancers whom they abducted. Then they went and returned to their territory, and rebuilt the towns, and lived in them. So the Israelites departed from there at that time by tribes and families, and they went out from there to their own territories. In those days there was no king in Israel; all the people did what was right in their own eyes.

The book of Judges tends not to be read or preached a great deal in many churches, or given much attention in many sets of Bible notes. There's a good reason for that: it is full of the most horrendous, unedifying tales of wickedness and violence. The story of the Benjaminites' abduction and forced marriage of young women from other tribes (and, indeed, of the other tribes' collaboration in it) is fairly typical, including a massacre of men, women and children a few verses before the passage we have read today. In this book, the Israelites have come a long way from the beauty of Eden and the royal vocation of humanity.

I write these notes and you read them (in all probability) in peace. I do not expect the people from the town up the road to sweep in, destroy my home and steal my children. Despite all that could be better in our country, we live, by and large, in peace and security. This is not because we are a different species from those who live in Syria, Afghanistan or a dozen other places torn by war. It is because, for all its flaws, we have a basically strong, basically trusted system of government, law and authority. Human communities, and therefore every individual human being, needs government and authority if they are to flourish. Without a king in Israel— without decent, lawful structures of authority—people will do what is right in their own eyes, and it will be the war of all against all. The book of Judges should be read as a terrible warning.

'We beseech thee also to defend all Christian Kings, Princes and Governors… that we may be godly and quietly governed'
(Book of Common Prayer).

PETER WADDELL

53

The vocation to rule

In your majesty ride on victoriously for the cause of truth and to defend the right; let your right hand teach you dread deeds. Your arrows are sharp in the heart of the king's enemies; the peoples fall under you. Your throne, O God, endures for ever and ever. Your royal sceptre is a sceptre of equity; you love righteousness and hate wickedness. Therefore God, your God, has anointed you with the oil of gladness beyond your companions.

Why do we have kings? Or, in a more democratic age, why do we have leaders? Why should anyone wish to be leader, and why should the rest of us consent to be led?

This psalm says something very simple, which is easily forgotten. The point of being king, or any kind of political leader, is to bring justice—to help righteousness to be done throughout the land and to fight against wickedness. That's what political leadership is for, just as nurses are for treating the sick and teachers for educating the young. Perhaps, as in education and medicine, we should recover the idea of leadership as vocation rather than ambition. We could think seriously about how we form candidates for political leadership, as we form medics, teachers, social workers and clergy—prioritising their spiritual and ethical foundations. We have become far too used to thinking of politics in terms of the struggle for the top job. We and our leaders would do well to remember the basics: it is not about whether John or Jane Smith gets the prize, but about how righteousness will flourish and wickedness be rebuked.

There's an ambiguity in the translation here: it's unclear whether we should read 'Your throne, O God, endures for ever' or 'Your throne is a throne of God; it endures for ever.' It's a good ambiguity, though, because it reminds us that all human authority is rooted in the divine authority, images the divine authority, and should do what the divine authority does. The only throne that truly lasts for ever belongs to God. All human leaders will one day kneel before it and give an account of their rule.

Lord, create a right spirit within all who would lead us.
May their thrones be rooted in yours.

PETER WADDELL

The beauty of kingship

The spirit of the Lord speaks through me, his word is upon my tongue. The God of Israel has spoken, the Rock of Israel has said to me: One who rules over people justly, ruling in the fear of God, is like the light of morning, like the sun rising on a cloudless morning, gleaming from the rain on the grassy land.

In his fantasy novel *Feet of Clay* (1996), Terry Pratchett writes, 'Whoever had created humanity had left in a major design flaw. It was its tendency to bend at the knees.' Pratchett was no fan of monarchy, and yet, as one of his republican characters observed, 'Royalty was like dandelions. No matter how many heads you chopped off, the roots were still there, waiting to spring up again.' Maybe there's a reason for that, and there's a hint of it in today's reading.

Despite the fact that monarchy can go wrong and become about extreme and unmerited privilege, at heart there is something beautiful about the idea—a beauty caught in these words from 2 Samuel. Isn't there something deeply attractive, deeply resonant at a heart-level, about the idea that what a country gathers around is rooted in something greater than a majority vote—that Government and Opposition are both involved in something bigger than partisan struggle, both belonging to a common national family and project? Her Majesty's Government and Her Majesty's Loyal Opposition: we belong in one community, gathered around a living, breathing symbol of unity and continuity. Something similar is represented by the office of bishops, for those churches that have them.

Perhaps that's why, no matter how far we have reduced the practical powers of our monarchy and how highly we value our democratic system, there remains an enduring attachment to the idea of royalty. How else to explain the resonance of stories like *The Lion King* or *The Lord of the Rings*? Deep down, something in us yearns for kingship, which summons our allegiance and to which we can bow the knee. We yearn for something that points beyond itself to our relationship with our Creator.

Lord God, create the beauty and simplicity of true allegiance to you within my heart.

PETER WADDELL

Beauty spoiled: kings and bandits

'He will take your daughters to be perfumers and cooks and bakers. He will take the best of your fields and vineyards and olive orchards and give them to his courtiers... He will take one-tenth of your flocks, and you shall be his slaves. And in that day you will cry out because of your king, whom you have chosen for yourselves; but the Lord will not answer you in that day.'

It might come as a surprise to the reader of these notes thus far, but personally I am rather ambivalent about the idea of monarchy. The Hebrew scriptures are emphatically so. Yes, they sing in praise of how good *good* kingship is, and they see it as making real in Israel's politics something of God's rule. On the other hand, they are fully aware of the way earthly kingship usually degenerates. For all the sentiment of the previous passages we have read, there is nothing less romantic than the view of kings that today's passage from 1 Samuel takes: they are just the biggest robber barons around, and they will prey on the poor. It is hard to deny that, in many times and places, that analysis has proved spot on.

Biblical people, then, must not be starry-eyed about kings and queens and all who serve in authority. The doctrine of original sin affects those institutions and individuals as much as it does all others. There is a tendency—a very strong and never-ceasing tendency—for power and the powerful to go wrong: they tend to get lost in power, to become arrogant, greedy and domineering. It is one of the most important reasons why our rulers stand in urgent need of our prayers, whether we approve of them or not. Arguably, indeed, one good reason for electing a head of state is that at least the poor sinner who is chosen will soon be removed from their position of extreme spiritual vulnerability.

The test of a monarch, president or prime minister—or of a manager, headteacher or parent—is whether they serve. Do they protect the poor and the weak? God alone commands our unconditional allegiance.

'Remove justice, and what are kingdoms but gangs of criminals on a large scale?' (Augustine, City of God IV:5.4)

PETER WADDELL

Beauty spoiled: kings and killing

In the spring of the year, the time when kings go out to battle, David sent Joab with his officers and all Israel with him; they ravaged the Ammonites, and besieged Rabbah. But David remained at Jerusalem. It happened, late one afternoon, when David rose from his couch and was walking about on the roof of the king's house, that he saw from the roof a woman bathing; the woman was very beautiful.

This is the beginning of the famous story of David and Bathsheba, in which the king arranges the death of his loyal commander to cover up the fact that he's been sleeping with that soldier's wife. King David may loom large in Israel's history and hope, and therefore in Christian theology, but no one could say that the scriptures attempt to airbrush his career. Cromwell famously asked for his portrait to be painted 'warts and all': David got similar treatment from the writers of the Bible.

Almost the saddest aspect of this story, though, is the way it starts: 'In the spring of the year, the time when kings go out to battle…' War: it's just what kings do. This is one of the gloomiest asides in the Bible. Just as the lambs come and the flowers bloom, powerful men quarrel and send others to die for them—to burn, rape and kill for them. Indeed, it has been persuasively suggested by some historians that one reason why Europe has enjoyed relative peace for a long, stable stretch is because its monarchies and autocracies have, on the whole, been replaced by democracies. If you want peace, the lesson appears to be, lose your kings.

Even our own very limited, very constitutional monarchy is implicated in all this. Elected governments take us to war now, but the deep royal involvement with all things military keeps alive the idea that national identity, national pride and patriotism are inextricably bound up with killing other people. Very few Christians are pacifist (though perhaps too few worry why not), but that identification should cause us all deep unease. Monarchy is not just a lovely thing. It's dangerous.

'They shall beat their swords into ploughshares, and their spears into pruning hooks; nation shall not lift up sword against nation, neither shall they learn war any more' (Micah 4:3–4).

PETER WADDELL

Why kings need folly

But when his heart was lifted up and his spirit was hardened so that he acted proudly, he was deposed from his kingly throne, and his glory was stripped from him. He was driven from human society, and his mind was made like that of an animal. His dwelling was with the wild asses, he was fed grass like oxen, and his body was bathed with the dew of heaven, until he learned that the Most High God has sovereignty over the kingdom of mortals, and sets over it whomsoever he will.

The king in question is Nebuchadnezzar, whom the Bible sees as having been raised to power by God but then, lost in his arrogance and pride, cast down by God to learn humility. Now Daniel repeats the warning to Nebuchadnezzar's son, Belshazzar, who has compounded his father's crime by using the sacred vessels looted from Jerusalem for his pagan banquet. Daniel is clear: Belshazzar, like all kings, holds his office on divine sufferance alone. If the monarch is there, in some sense, by divine providence and permission, this is not a licence to do what he or she pleases. To serve at God's pleasure means to serve under judgement.

Arguably, one of the most significant steps in the development of European fascism in the 20th century was the erosion, or suppression, of the sense of the ridiculous. It's not just that dictators don't like to be laughed at; it's more that whole cultures lost sight of the sheer absurdity of jumped-up little men presuming to near-divine status. In some ways, a robust faith in God is one of the strong roots of comedy and freedom: if God is God, then there is something more than faintly ridiculous about all human power and glory. The right response to fascism—before we have to go to war—is really to mock it. And when a society is frightened to laugh or be lauhed at, alarm bells should start ringing!

'The kings of the earth set themselves, and the rulers take counsel together, against the Lord and his Anointed… He who sits in the heavens laughs; the Lord has them in derision' (Psalm 2:2, 4).

PETER WADDELL

Pray for your rulers

First of all, then, I urge that supplications, prayers, intercessions, and thanksgivings should be made for everyone, for kings and all who are in high positions, so that we may lead a quiet and peaceable life in all godliness and dignity. This is right and acceptable in the sight of God our Saviour, who desires everyone to be saved and to come to the knowledge of the truth.

To pray for the monarch or the government is not a sign that one approves of either. Prayer is not about approval, but love. We pray for the monarch and her advisers not because we support them but because they are human beings whom God loves and wants to come to a knowledge of the truth. What is more, they are in a position that is at once immensely important and dangerously spiritually exposed. If we believe in prayer at all, they need our prayers.

What do we ask? First, what we ask for anyone—that they might know the truth and be saved, that Jesus may be very real to them, and that their lives may be lived in an ever closer union with him. Imagine what a difference it would make to government, before any question of policy arises, if the powerful were constantly striving to become personally more like Jesus, transformed by the Spirit into his likeness. They would be utterly selfless and honest; they would forgive their enemies; they would serve the weak and vulnerable.

Then we ask for that which belongs specifically to their political calling—for the gifts of wisdom and skill, to know the best way to translate their Jesus-instincts into law and policy. The ideas they come up with may seem strange, or even outrageous to us—in which case there are at least two sharp questions. One: what makes us think that we are the best judges of how to translate Christian principle ito political practice? Two: how do we resist the temptation to demonise our opponents? The answer to the first is self-examination and study; the answer to the second is prayer.

Father, we pray for our leaders. Keep them near to you, and make them like your Son Jesus in all that they do and plan. Amen

PETER WADDELL

A sword-from-stone moment

'You have heard that it was said, "An eye for an eye and a tooth for a tooth." But I say to you, Do not resist an evildoer. But if anyone strikes you on the right cheek, turn the other also; and if anyone wants to sue you and take your coat, give your cloak as well; and if anyone forces you to go one mile, go also the second mile.'

The legend tells us that it was when young Arthur drew the sword from the stone that his claim to kingship was vindicated. This was the boy whom the land had been waiting for: other pretenders had come and gone, but in this boy hope and history rhymed. Things finally came right.

This moment from Matthew's Gospel has a similar resonance. Jesus stands on the mountain, as Moses had stood long ago, and simply declares, 'You have heard it said… But I say to you…' That is an astonishing claim, a sword-from-the-stone moment. Jesus stands as the new lawgiver, who on his own authority sets out how Israel is to be. He stands as a true king, one who does not appeal to academic qualification, military power or religious sanction for his claim, but simply presents himself and commands his subjects' allegiance.

And that command finds a response in innumerable human hearts. Jesus' royal authority resonates well beyond Christianity: there are many who doubt or deny the church's theological claims about him, who nevertheless instinctively recognise that here is moral authority. Here indeed is the way, the truth, the life: in some sense, Jesus lays a powerful summons on each and every one of us.

It is also a summons—not a proposal for discussion or the opening gambit in a negotiation. We need to be very careful about this idea because it is so easily abused, but what comes across clearly in this reading is, above all, the sense of authority. Jesus seeks not our approval or agreement, but our obedience. And he is entitled to it: we were made for this allegiance. The knee is indeed meant to bend.

'What moral teacher of men ever showed less anxiety
to commend himself to majorities?' (Charles Gore).

PETER WADDELL

Power which will not overpower

Then they brought the colt to Jesus and threw their cloaks on it; and he sat on it. Many people spread their cloaks on the road, and others spread leafy branches that they had cut in the fields. Then those who went ahead and those who followed were shouting, 'Hosanna! Blessed is the one who comes in the name of the Lord! Blessed is the coming kingdom of our ancestor David!'

Arthur may have pulled a sword from the stone, but the striking thing about Jesus' kingship is that (except in the curious Luke 22:38) swords do not appear to have played much of a role in it. Swords were for other people—the Roman overlords and their collaborators, and those who were militantly opposed to them. At this pivotal moment in the Gospel story, which marks Jesus' most explicit claim to kingship (for that is what this palm-waving procession into Jerusalem meant), all the Gospels agree that he did it in a decidedly non-militaristic way. He was riding a donkey—slow, humble and unassuming. This was a king who brought no bloodshed.

So there is a real paradox here. We saw yesterday that Jesus' claim is imperious: it brooks no negotiation; it seeks no response but unreserved, knee-bending allegiance and obedience. This is your king, not your chum. And yet, his claim is without violence: it will not force. Jesus will not compel his subjects. He does not want subjects: 'I do not call you servants any longer… but I have called you friends' (John 15:15). He has ultimate, overwhelming authority—and yet he will not overwhelm. This king wants the free response of love, not the cringing obeisance of fear.

That is true, but we often say it too quickly today. It seems to me that the church today is more likely to make the mistake of treating Jesus like a cuddly friend than to see him as an imposing tyrant. Both approaches are mistakes, but might we need reminding that the first is just as bad as the second?

'The fear of the Lord is the beginning of wisdom' (Proverbs 9:10) and yet 'perfect love casts out fear' (1 John 4:18): how do you reconcile those two thoughts?

PETER WADDELL

Very sensible betrayals

Now it was the day of Preparation for the Passover; and it was about noon. He said to the Jews, 'Here is your King!' They cried out, 'Away with him! Away with him! Crucify him!' Pilate asked them, 'Shall I crucify your King?' The chief priests answered, 'We have no king but the emperor.' Then he handed him over to them to be crucified.

There are moments in the Gospels when the account seems so theologically profound that we might wonder whether it can also be historically accurate. This is one of those moments. Can the chief priests really have said so simply, so unequivocally, something that they may have thought secretly but that every good Jew would have denied: 'We have no king but the emperor'? God was the King of Israel, the priests his representatives: for them to condemn themselves so frankly here is startling.

On the other hand, why doubt John's historicity when we know from our own time how readily God's people find themselves in similarly startling circumstances? The use of a nuclear missile is, by any standard of Christian reasoning, whether in the pacifist or the just-war tradition, an abhorrent crime, the most spectacular offence against the divine majesty. Yet our bishops go and bless Trident submarines; and, whatever rationalisation is offered, the picture is just as startling as those high priests pledging allegiance to the emperor. Indeed, it's the same picture.

The thing is, there *are* rationalisations in both cases. High priests should care about peace and stability. It is not unChristian to think that national defence is a good thing, and should we not pray for our sailors? The church cannot hide away in useless purity, and the state is not the devil: collaboration is not a dirty word but a part of mission. So the question is not whether to collaborate but how to know when collaboration has gone disastrously wrong, when working with the emperor has become rejection of God. It is always a difficult call, but a good clue that we have got it wrong is when we find ourselves crucifying the innocent.

'See, I am sending you out like sheep into the midst of wolves; so be wise as serpents, and innocent as doves' (Matthew 10:16).

PETER WADDELL

Stronger than hammers and nails

Pilate also had an inscription written and put on the cross. It read, 'Jesus of Nazareth, the King of the Jews.' Many of the Jews read this inscription, because the place where Jesus was crucified was near the city; and it was written in Hebrew, in Latin, and in Greek. Then the chief priests of the Jews said to Pilate, 'Do not write, "The King of the Jews", but, "This man said, I am King of the Jews."' Pilate answered, 'What I have written I have written.'

There's an ancient tradition that Pontius Pilate eventually became a Christian and a martyr. Sadly, like many such traditions, its historicity is deeply suspect. Undoubtedly, though, John does present Pilate here as offering unwitting testimony to Jesus. The sign he mounted over the cross of Jesus was meant to taunt and humiliate him, his followers and all the Jews, to rub their faces in the brute reality of Roman power. For John, of course, it tells the simple truth: here indeed is the King of the Jews. Here is the one in whom all those ancient promises about peace and justice come true.

The ironies pile up. Pilate was charged with the maintenance of Roman peace and justice, and he did it in the way empires, kings and governors generally do—with hammers and nails and violence. Jesus was charged with divine judgement. It was his vocation to bring justice in God's way, which in scripture seldom means simply the destruction of the wicked. There is always a bigger purpose in view—the setting right of things, the bringing of peace rather than death. And he does it in God's way, through being crucified, through absorbing all the violence and hate of the world, holding it within himself and rising through it to heal.

Christians are charged to be like him—to bring peace and justice through the way of suffering, of loving sacrifice. These ethics are based on the theology that, ultimately, the most royal sovereignty of all has nothing to do with violence and everything to do with love. That's the gospel in a nutshell.

'Love is the only force capable of transforming an enemy to a friend'
(Martin Luther King, Jr).

PETER WADDELL

The day of justice

Then I saw heaven opened, and there was a white horse! Its rider is called Faithful and True, and in righteousness he judges and makes war… From his mouth comes a sharp sword with which to strike down the nations, and he will rule them with a rod of iron; he will tread the wine press of the fury of the wrath of God the Almighty. On his robe and on his thigh he has a name inscribed, 'King of kings and Lord of lords'.

How can we reconcile this image with the way of the cross? What has happened to the God who will not force, who will win only through love?

It is not entirely clear that the two pictures are reconcilable. The Jesus of the book of Revelation, it seems, is one who, in the end, *will* use force: the wicked, if they will not turn and be forgiven, will be destroyed. Nor can we say that this picture is merely 'according to Revelation', a book whose authority has often been disputed (Martin Luther attempted to remove it from the Bible). The Jesus of the Gospels can be equally fierce: 'You that are accursed, depart from me into the eternal fire prepared for the devil and his angels' (Matthew 25:41). A deep tension between the final justice of God, which must mean doom for the wicked, and the suffering love of God for all his creatures, runs throughout the New Testament.

It is a tension that we should not defuse quickly. Much contemporary Christianity dislikes the idea of a punishing, vengeful God—and undoubtedly, in the past, preachers took far too great a relish in presenting him as such. Nonetheless, what other response is adequate to the crimes committed against his beloved creatures? How is God meant to deal with the unrepentant killers and torturers and abusers? Everything in us cries out for justice, and yet (in our better moments) simultaneously for mercy. It is a tension beyond human resolution: all we can hope is that with God all things are possible. We may hope for the wicked, that God's justice might mean their healing. We cannot presume to know it.

'Mercy and truth are met together; righteousness
and peace have kissed each other' (Psalm 85:10, KJV).

PETER WADDELL

In the end, the beginning

Nothing accursed will be found there any more. But the throne of God and of the Lamb will be in it, and his servants will worship him; they will see his face, and his name will be on their foreheads. And there will be no more night; they need no light of lamp or sun, for the Lord God will be their light, and they will reign for ever and ever.

We began in Genesis, with the royal vocation of men and women made in God's image, as kings and queens of creation. We end in the heavenly city and its throne room where the long saga climaxes—where Jesus raises men and women to be what they were made to be, to share in his kingship for ever.

What does that actually mean? The resurrection is beyond words: to describe it is like staring into the sun. That's why Saul, when he met the risen Jesus on the Damascus road, saw a blinding flash of light. Anyone who says too much risks making a fool of themselves. Yet we can say a little, as Paul did, and we can start with the idea of our royal vocation, reigning in the kingdom.

To be kings and queens of creation means to be free—free of all that hurts and oppresses us now. Violence, hate, greed, all that is wicked within and without, will be burnt up in love. And this is not just good news for us. Paul says in Romans 8:19 that the whole creation 'waits with eager longing for the revealing of the children of God', for our freedom and glory. It waits because, then, we will do what we were made to do: we will be the ones through whom everything else is made right and comes to its fullness. That's what being kings and queens is all about. The world will sing, in, through and because of us.

It sounds absurd because it is beyond language, but that does not mean it is not real. It is our royal destiny. Hallelujah!

Nearer and nearer draws the time,
the time that shall surely be,
when the earth shall be filled with the glory of God
as the waters cover the sea.

Arthur Aigner (1849–1919)

PETER WADDELL

Philippians: letter of joy

It is a joy for me to be writing in *New Daylight* for the first time and an equal joy to have been asked to write on Paul's Letter to the Philippians, which is a letter of joy. (Yes, you've got it—the key word here is joy!)

The words 'joy' and 'rejoice' together appear 14 times in this short letter. This is perhaps surprising, since Paul is writing from prison, possibly in Ephesus in modern-day Turkey. Nevertheless, by the grace of God he is able to rejoice under the most trying circumstances, and the letter will for ever stand as a tribute to the apostle's attitude to his sufferings. Paul rejoices in the continued advance of the gospel despite his imprisonment, in his special partnership with the Philippians, in the recovery from the near-fatal illness of Epaphroditus (who brings him gifts from Philippi and returns there carrying this letter), and in anticipation of Christ's return when the believers shall be saved.

A brief background summary may be helpful here. We know from Acts that Paul, while on his second missionary journey in about AD50, had a vision of 'a man of Macedonia' (Acts 16:9) who pleaded with him to come and help them. Interpreting this as a summons from God, Paul and his companions set sail across the Aegean Sea from Troas (near the site of ancient Troy, in modern Turkey), arriving at Neapolis (now Kavala in northern Greece), the seaport of Philippi. Philippi was a Roman colony, which means that it was governed by Rome, not Macedonia, and was subject to Roman law. Here Paul established one or a number of house churches, his first in Europe.

Some years later, perhaps in the mid-50s, the Christians in Philippi heard of Paul's imprisonment and responded with prayers to gain his release and gifts to supply his needs. These gifts were delivered to Paul by Epaphroditus, who then became seriously ill. Upon his recovery, Paul sent him back to Philippi along with this letter.

So let's journey back in time to the Roman Empire, to the Greece and Turkey of the mid-first century, and see how Paul's words can speak into our lives today.

TIM HEATON

Greetings

Paul and Timothy, servants of Christ Jesus, To all God's holy people in Christ Jesus at Philippi, together with the overseers and deacons: Grace and peace to you from God our Father and the Lord Jesus Christ.

Paul's opening salutation to 'God's holy people' (v. 1) at Philippi, by which he means all the Christians there, ends with a wonderful blessing of grace and peace. I remember reading the acronym GRACE: God's Riches At Christ's Expense. It sums up perfectly the divine favour and goodwill in which we stand, won for us through the cross and resurrection of Jesus.

The few converts left behind after a visit lasting only 'several days' (Acts 16:12) have thrived, flourished and multiplied. Now, just a few years later, they exist as a viable church. They have adopted a coherent structure and appointed local leaders. These 'overseers' (leaders whom the church much later came to call bishops) and 'deacons' are not identified, although it would not be preposterous to suggest that one of the overseers might have been Lydia (Acts 16:40).

Paul's protégé and trusted companion Timothy is named as co-sender of this letter. They were together when the church at Philippi was established, and Paul calls him a fellow 'servant' of Christ. Servanthood can sometimes be hard for us to accept; we don't always like to think of ourselves as being anyone's servant. Perhaps we confuse it with 'doormat'! I remember planning a funeral service and reading to the family a prayer I was going to include that begins, 'Father in heaven, we give you thanks for your servant N...' They said, 'It's very nice, but can you take out the word "servant"?'

It was hard for them to think of their late mother in this way, but Paul's characterisation of himself and Timothy as 'servants' of Christ—literally slaves, given wholly and completely to the service of God—becomes, as we shall see, an important theme of the letter.

God of grace and peace, I pray that you will pour an abundance of your blessings upon all those whom I love and with whom I work, today and always.

TIM HEATON

Joy in prison

I thank my God every time I remember you, constantly praying with joy in every one of my prayers for all of you, because of your sharing in the gospel from the first day until now. I am confident of this, that the one who began a good work among you will bring it to completion by the day of Jesus Christ. It is right for me to think this way about all of you, because you hold me in your heart, for all of you share in God's grace with me, both in my imprisonment and in the defence and confirmation of the gospel.

Here is the first incidence of the word 'joy' (v. 4) in a letter that is rich in joy. Paul writes that he is in prison (v. 7) but does not say where. He was not incarcerated for criminal behaviour: rather, he was what we would call today a 'political prisoner' or 'prisoner of conscience', someone whose detention has been imposed in violation of their freedom of thought, conscience or religion. Often such people have opposed or criticised their government, and frequently they are detained without trial.

As I write this, Christians in China are enduring a government-backed cross demolition campaign. More than 2000 church crosses have been destroyed and many church buildings have been torn down. Pastor Zhang was imprisoned for seven months because of his non-violent opposition to this campaign, convicted on a trumped-up charge of 'stealing, spying, buying, or illegally providing state secrets or intelligence to entities outside China'. Many other church leaders are in detention, waiting to receive an official charge.

Such was Paul's imprisonment, which was 'for Christ' (1:13), but it results in the further spread of the gospel, and this is a cause for joy. Paradoxically, joy may also be the outcome of suffering and sorrow for Christ's sake, since it is, for Paul, less an emotion than a state of mind, something that can be cultivated.

God of joy, may joy be at the heart of my Christian life,
whatever the circumstances, and may my service be given gladly,
not grudgingly, and with rejoicing.

TIM HEATON

Life or death?

It is my eager expectation and hope that I will not be put to shame in any way, but that by my speaking with all boldness, Christ will be exalted now as always in my body, whether by life or by death. For to me, living is Christ and dying is gain. If I am to live in the flesh, that means fruitful labour for me; and I do not know which I prefer. I am hard pressed between the two: my desire is to depart and be with Christ, for that is far better; but to remain in the flesh is more necessary for you.

Despite his imprisonment, Paul is able to remain joyful, and the secret of his rejoicing is his fellowship with the Lord who is the centre of his being, whatever the future may hold.

I've been in prison as a Prison Visitor and I also ran the Samaritans' 'Listener Scheme' in the same prison for a number of years, so I have a fair idea of what conditions are like in our prisons today. I wouldn't agree with those who say that prison life is too soft, easy and comfortable. Whatever your thoughts on that, however, it is hard to imagine today the conditions that Paul was living under. Prisons in the Roman Empire were not meant for lengthy incarcerations; rather, they were filthy, rat-infested dungeons in which prisoners were held until sentenced, either to freedom or execution. Conditions were so inhumane that no one could have survived them for long. Prisoners' welfare was not a matter for the state, and, without family and friends bringing food and other necessities, a prisoner would soon die. Given these conditions, the gifts brought by Epaphroditus would have been not just thoughtful presents but the difference between life and death: food and water, clean clothing, a basin for washing. It's hardly any wonder, then, that Paul debated with himself whether living or dying would be better.

O merciful God… Whether I live or die, I am with you, and you, my God, are with me. Lord, I wait for your salvation and for your kingdom.

Dietrich Bonhoeffer, 'Prayers for fellow prisoners, Christmas 1943'

TIM HEATON

Humility

If then there is any encouragement in Christ, any consolation from love, any sharing in the Spirit, any compassion and sympathy, make my joy complete: be of the same mind, having the same love, being in full accord and of one mind. Do nothing from selfish ambition or conceit, but in humility regard others as better than yourselves. Let each of you look not to your own interests, but to the interests of others.

There's a piece of paper pinned on the cork board above my desk that says, 'Always consider others to be better than yourself.' It has been there for many years. Having read Philippians 2:3 long ago, I wanted always to be reminded of it. I need to be reminded of it, every minute of every day, because humility is not a quality that comes easily or naturally to me.

The importance of humility springs from its being part of the character of God. Wherever humility is found in the Bible, it is praised, and God's blessing is frequently poured upon those who possess it. It means having a modest view of one's own importance and is the very opposite of pride, which was the 'original sin' of Adam and Eve in the story of Genesis 3. They thought they could go it alone without God, ignoring God in the world that God had made, striving for the fulfilment of life through the enrichment of their own egos—but they couldn't. Pride came before the fall.

I love to see humility in others. I see it from time to time in people who have done great things, and it invariably brings tears to my eyes. We can see it also in the encounters of everyday life. Today, whoever you meet and whatever befalls, whether you are a viscount or a valet, the maid or the marchioness, remember humility. Remember to regard others as better than yourself, and I shall try to do it too. It will make us much better people, I promise, and it is the hallmark of true discipleship.

Loving God, give me a humble heart, to put the interests of others before my own, and the humility always to regard others as better than myself.

TIM HEATON

Humiliation

Let the same mind be in you that was in Christ Jesus, who, though he was in the form of God, did not regard equality with God as something to be exploited, but emptied himself, taking the form of a slave, being born in human likeness. And being found in human form, he humbled himself and became obedient to the point of death—even death on a cross.

There are two outstanding features of Paul's letter to the Philippians. The first is what it reveals about the apostle's attitude to his sufferings, which has made it a source of great comfort to many Christians in their own suffering over two millennia. The second is the great passage in 2:5–11, which we begin today and conclude tomorrow.

The words from 'who, though he was in the form of God' onwards are widely regarded to be an early 'Christ hymn'. That is to say, these are not Paul's own words; he is quoting material from an early Christian liturgy, perhaps modified slightly. It is called a 'hymn' because originally it would have been sung; at a time when few people could read but many loved to sing, it was natural for the basic tenets of faith to be embedded in memorable worship songs.

This first part of the hymn tells of Christ's life and, more especially, his death. It speaks of his death in terms of the submission and obedience that are characteristic of a slave. It emphasises his crucifixion, which was a particularly cruel form of punishment reserved for slaves, traitors, brigands, and others of little or no status. The cross was the ultimate symbol of rejection, degradation and humiliation.

We sometimes say we feel 'totally humiliated' after we have been made to feel ashamed or foolish in front of others, but real humiliation is the complete loss of dignity and self-esteem. In the film *Bonhoeffer— Agent of Grace* (2000), Dietrich is shown going to the gallows naked, just as Jesus, Son of the Most High God, probably went to the cross. Explanations seem impossible. For now, let Calvary tell its own heart-piercing tale.

Suffering God, as your church remembers today Peter and Paul, inspire me by their teaching and example, and strengthen me to witness to your truth.

TIM HEATON

Exaltation

Therefore God also highly exalted him and gave him the name that is above every name, so that at the name of Jesus every knee should bend, in heaven and on earth and under the earth, and every tongue should confess that Jesus Christ is Lord, to the glory of God the Father.

Whereas the first part of this ancient hymn speaks of Christ's life and death in terms of slavery, this second part speaks of his resurrection and ascension in terms of the status and power accorded to a master.

Jesus' *kenosis* or 'self-emptying' (2:7) was the supreme example of humility. He voluntarily set aside his omnipotence in sharing the human condition and suffering a humiliating death on a cross. We must be clear that Christ remained at all times fully divine: he was able to turn water into wine, yet on another occasion refused to turn stones into loaves of bread.

What follows humiliation is exaltation, and the word 'therefore' (v. 9) suggests that the latter happens as a direct result of the former. It is precisely because Jesus humbled himself as a slave in this world that God gave him the name that is above every name—Lord. Jesus emptied himself of his divine power and glory by becoming human, only to receive it back in the resurrection. In a marvellous reversal, the one who dispossesses everything comes, in the end, to possess all things as Lord.

The way of the cross is not an end in itself but a stage on the way to resurrection and eternal life. If Jesus found glory through suffering, then that is the path to glory for his followers. Suffering is, in some sense, a sharing in the suffering of Christ, to be accepted—joyfully in Paul's case—as part of the road to the kingdom of God. So the Philippians are called to humility and slave-like service, to put aside self-interest for pain and loss, not just for the sake of it but because this is the way to the presence of God. They won't just share the suffering; they'll share the glory too.

Jesus Christ, risen Lord, may I enter into the mystery of your suffering and, by following in your way, come to share in your glory.

TIM HEATON

Good works

Therefore, my beloved, just as you have always obeyed me, not only in my presence, but much more now in my absence, work out your own salvation with fear and trembling; for it is God who is at work in you, enabling you both to will and to work for his good pleasure. Do all things without murmuring and arguing, so that you may be blameless and innocent, children of God without blemish in the midst of a crooked and perverse generation, in which you shine like stars in the world.

Paul's words in verse 12, 'work out your own salvation with fear and trembling', are really interesting. They appear at first sight to contradict everything he says in his letters about salvation being the free gift of a loving God. He teaches time and again that we are saved by grace through faith, not because we do good deeds and stay out of trouble. While we will all be judged, the living and the dead, Paul believed that sinners (and we are all indicted) who trust in the perfect merit and finished work of Christ as Saviour have a guarantee of acquittal. Christ's faithfulness, his perfect obedience in life and death, are imputed to us here and now and will stand to our account on judgement day. The verdict has already been announced in the death and resurrection of Jesus.

Then why does Paul now tell the Philippians to 'work out' their own salvation, as if it somehow depended on human effort? I think the answer is that he understands good works to be the natural consequence of faith. He believes good works to be a gift of God in creation (Ephesians 2:10) and the direct fruit of regeneration by the Holy Spirit (Colossians 1:10). So he calls the Philippians simply to live each day in the reality of what God has already done, to walk in the light, to labour in obedience and reverent fear of God (that is, awe) in response to God's gift of salvation; but to know that their works are God's works and will not be counted to their credit on judgement day.

Awesome God, work in me through your indwelling Spirit, that I may walk in the light of your salvation and respond by being worthy of it.

TIM HEATON

Poured out

It is by your holding fast to the word of life that I can boast on the day of Christ that I did not run in vain or labour in vain. But even if I am being poured out as a libation over the sacrifice and the offering of your faith, I am glad and rejoice with all of you—and in the same way you also must be glad and rejoice with me. I hope in the Lord Jesus to send Timothy to you soon, so that I may be cheered by news of you. I have no one like him who will be genuinely concerned for your welfare.

Having already pointed to Jesus as an example to the Philippians of looking not to their own interests but to the interests of others (2:5–11), Paul now offers himself as a model by referring to his own work among them.

Have you ever felt totally spent and completely drained? I hope you haven't routinely felt like this in your service of Christ, but you might have experienced it at some time of crisis in your life. 'Poured out as a libation' (v. 17) is a vivid image of a drink-offering from sacrificial ritual. Here Paul is saying that Christ's self-emptying has become the form of his own existence. He has emptied himself in Christ-like service to them, and they should therefore respond by 'pouring out' themselves in self-sacrificial love and service to each other.

Timothy, also, is an example to them of 'the same mind that was in Christ' (2:5), of a life lived for others. He is 'genuinely concerned' for the Philippians' welfare and, like Paul, his service is defined by their needs, not by his own desires. Just as Jesus himself took 'the form of a slave' (2:7), so Paul and Timothy—in the imitation of Christ—have slaved not for their own glory but for the good of the Philippians. In tomorrow's passage, Epaphroditus is commended too.

What will you do today for the body of Christ in your time and place, and for the wider community?

Father of all, help me at all times to have a genuine concern for the welfare of others, and to put their needs above my own desires.

TIM HEATON

Challenge and danger

[Epaphroditus] was indeed so ill that he nearly died. But God had mercy on him, and not only on him but on me also, so that I would not have one sorrow after another. I am the more eager to send him, therefore, in order that you may rejoice at seeing him again, and that I may be less anxious. Welcome him then in the Lord with all joy, and honour such people, because he came close to death for the work of Christ, risking his life to make up for those services that you could not give me.

Paul is able to rejoice in the recovery of Epaphroditus, the Philippians' emissary, from a near-fatal illness in spite of his own sorrow and anxiety. It is possible that Epaphroditus succumbed to this sickness during his visits to the disease-ridden dungeon where Paul was being held. He will have spent several days there, comforting and encouraging Paul, and also—we can presume—taking down this letter from Paul's dictation. (We know from Galatians 6:11 that Paul did not have a scribal hand, so it is possible that Epaphroditus made himself useful in this way.) Whether it was as a direct result of these visits to the prison that 'he nearly died' (v. 27), we can't be sure, but it is clear that Paul is immensely grateful to him for ministering to his needs, and now plans to send him back to Philippi with this letter.

Just before these verses, Paul calls Epaphroditus 'my fellow soldier' (2:25), a military metaphor that suggests the struggle and danger inherent in their missionary work. Though we might not face the same dangers, Philippians serves to remind us that being on the outside of mainstream culture is the normal status of the church. Mission in a largely unreceptive world has been part of the Christian story in every age. It is no less true today, and we should take encouragement from the fact that although Paul and his co-workers met with challenge and danger, their missionary efforts, thanks be to God, bore much fruit. Be heartened that yours will too.

God of mission, give me strength and courage to play my part in the spread of the gospel among those with whom I live and work.

TIM HEATON

Breaking with the past

Beware of the dogs, beware of the evil workers, beware of those who mutilate the flesh! For it is we who are the circumcision, who worship in the Spirit of God and boast in Christ Jesus and have no confidence in the flesh—even though I, too, have reason for confidence in the flesh. If anyone else has reason to be confident in the flesh, I have more: circumcised on the eighth day, a member of the people of Israel, of the tribe of Benjamin, a Hebrew born of Hebrews; as to the law, a Pharisee; as to zeal, a persecutor of the church; as to righteousness under the law, blameless.

The tone of the letter changes here as Paul warns the Philippians of some rival missionaries whose ideas pose a danger to them. It seems that these were some Jewish converts to Christianity who were insisting that Gentile converts should be circumcised. Paul abhors this as 'a righteousness… that comes from the law' (3:9), which is in direct opposition to his teaching of righteousness conferred by faith in Christ's death and resurrection.

Paul speaks against circumcision as one of the circumcised. Moreover, he recites his Jewish credentials in such a way as to suggest that he is more Jewish than most. He also doesn't want to sweep his inglorious past as a persecutor of Christians under the carpet, and reminds the Philippians of it as an example of his persistent and fervent devotion to a cause.

It is important that we don't forget Paul's previous life as Saul before his dramatic conversion. We shouldn't forget because it reminds us that no one is beyond the redeeming power of Christ. No one, however bad they are and whatever they have done in the past, is beyond the compass of God's grace. Paul was the villain of the story who became its hero, the sinner who became a saint. He went from being a stranger to Christ—even an enemy of Christ—to being captivated by him, and he shows us what Christ can do through a life surrendered to his Lordship.

Transforming God, help me to grow in the grace and knowledge of your Son Jesus Christ, which is what you long for in me and all your children.

TIM HEATON

Pressing onwards

I want to know Christ and the power of his resurrection and the sharing of his sufferings by becoming like him in his death, if somehow I may attain the resurrection from the dead. Not that I have already obtained this or have already reached the goal; but I press on to make it my own, because Christ Jesus has made me his own. Beloved, I do not consider that I have made it my own; but this one thing I do: forgetting what lies behind and straining forward to what lies ahead, I press on toward the goal for the prize of the heavenly call of God in Christ Jesus.

Being a Christian is a process rather than a finished state, a continual movement into a deeper knowledge of God and a richer experience of his love. Paul draws his imagery from the athletic arena, but 'pressing on toward the goal' (v. 14) is also the language of pilgrimage.

Like the story of salvation itself, which has always been told in the context of a deep emptiness and yearning, pilgrimage stems from an aching and longing to be nearer to God. The physical act of movement is seen to aid an inward journey of closer encounter with God, a voyage of inner transformation that brings us nearer to our true and eternal home. Pilgrimage is a metaphor for life, and life as a pathway ends with the culminating experience of being united with God. Life is a journey crowned with a goal, and the prize is the God from whom we have come and to whom we shall return.

Since the Middle Ages, the pilgrimage to Rome—to the tombs of St Peter and St Paul—has ranked second in the trio of so-called 'great pilgrimages' (between those to the Holy Sepulchre in Jerusalem and the shrine of St James the Great at Santiago de Compostela in north-west Spain). These sacred places, which are to be found at the end of long, arduous and sometimes dangerous journeys, are symbols of the 'heavenly city' (Hebrews 11:16) and of the culmination of the pilgrim's life and his or her union with God.

Creator God, source of my life and goal of my life,
sustain me on my earthly pilgrimage to my heavenly home.

TIM HEATON

Citizens of heaven

Brothers and sisters, join in imitating me, and observe those who live according to the example you have in us. For many live as enemies of the cross of Christ; I have often told you of them, and now I tell you even with tears. Their end is destruction; their god is the belly; and their glory is in their shame; their minds are set on earthly things. But our citizenship is in heaven, and it is from there that we are expecting a Saviour, the Lord Jesus Christ.

For a second time Paul presents himself and his co-workers to the Philippians as examples to be imitated (v. 17) and a pattern for Christian living. Positive role models are important. Who are, or have been, the most influential role models in your life? Pause here for a moment to think about that and give thanks to God for them today.

Paul's reference to those who 'live as enemies of the cross of Christ' (v. 18) could refer to some wayward Christians (see, for example, 1 Corinthians 6:12–20) but more probably, given what follows, to the pagans of Rome and her empire. Paul carried the gospel thousands of miles on Roman roads built for military conquest, and his activism was perceived by the authorities as a threat. Philippians often reads as a political manifesto of a radically alternate lifestyle, and here we have a prime instance of a subversive text that challenges the very foundations of the empire.

Because Philippi was a Roman colony, its people had Roman citizenship. Throughout the empire, the emperor or 'Caesar' was hailed as saviour and lord, even a god. (Whereas Jesus refused divine honours, there is only self-aggrandisement for Caesar!) Paul has already proclaimed a Lord superior to the emperor—the Lord Jesus, to whom 'every knee should bend' (2:10). Now he tells the Roman citizens of Philippi that their 'citizenship is in heaven, and it is from there that we are expecting a Saviour, the Lord Jesus Christ' (v. 20). No wonder he found himself in prison so often!

God of the nations, today there are new empires built on militarism, terror, oppression and exploitation. I pray for your kingdom of justice, equality, compassion and peace.

TIM HEATON

A final plea

Therefore, my brothers and sisters, whom I love and long for, my joy and crown, stand firm in the Lord in this way, my beloved. I urge Euodia and I urge Syntyche to be of the same mind in the Lord. Yes, and I ask you also, my loyal companion, help these women, for they have struggled beside me in the work of the gospel, together with Clement and the rest of my co-workers, whose names are in the book of life.

Paul seems to have a strong bond with the Philippians and a particular affection for them. His language and the gentle tone of the whole letter convey clearly the special relationship he has with the community. It is, in the end, a letter of friendship and fellowship, full of emotional warmth and tenderness. But fellowship, as we have seen throughout, means more to Paul than simply comradeship, companionship and the group solidarity that springs from shared work: it is expressed most fully in service to one another.

His earlier exhortation to the Philippians to have 'the same mind that was in Christ' (2:5) is now directed specifically to two women, Euodia and Syntyche, begging them 'to be of the same mind in the Lord' (v. 2). We can't know for sure exactly what has gone on here, but clearly something has been brought to Paul's notice, presumably by Epaphroditus. Given the emerging theme of the letter, we might hazard a guess that these two women, who were among the leaders of the church, were vying for power and status, concerned for their own interests rather than the interests of others.

Whatever the precise details, they have clearly fallen short of having the mind of Jesus. But let's not be too hard on them. Leadership is tough in any walk of life, and we should be thankful for all who offer to serve in this way—and pray for them (1 Timothy 2:1–2). All we need to remember here is that Christian love looks first of all to the needs of others. Self-interest has no place in the body of Christ.

Humble God, I pray today for the leaders of my own church, that they may minister with humility and not count themselves above others.

TIM HEATON

Rejoice in the Lord

Rejoice in the Lord always; again I will say, Rejoice. Let your gentleness be known to everyone. The Lord is near. Do not worry about anything, but in everything by prayer and supplication with thanksgiving let your requests be made known to God. And the peace of God, which surpasses all understanding, will guard your hearts and your minds in Christ Jesus.

With a final flurry of rejoicing, Paul draws his letter to a close (although he finishes by offering his full and formal thanks for the Philippians' gifts). As a letter of friendship written in response to prayers and gifts received from a church community with whom he has a special relationship, it unfolds as an extended demonstration of how Christian fellowship—service to one another—should shape the community's identity. Epaphroditus, on behalf of the Philippians, had clearly shown this service towards Paul, but there is more than a hint that 'selfish ambition or conceit' (2:3) had begun to take hold in some of the believers and was in danger of tainting the whole community.

Philippians is one of the greatest 'thank you' letters ever written. The pearl within it is the early Christ-hymn in 2:6–11, which expands the earliest and most basic Christian confession of faith, 'Jesus Christ is Lord', reaching back to the incarnation and forward to the eschatological future. It can lay claim to be one of the most-discussed passages in the whole Bible, and will for ever remain in the forefront of New Testament studies for what it reveals about the person of Christ and the nature and scope of Christian salvation. Jesus is held up as the exemplar of humility and self-emptying service, an example to be followed by the Philippians and the pattern on which they should base their lives. Paul then offers himself, Timothy and Epaphroditus as models to be imitated, and ends with a specific appeal to two individuals to follow these examples.

All that remains is for us, too, to try to follow them in our own time and place and, by our own example, encourage others to do the same.

Heavenly Father, bring the mind of Christ into being in me
and let it govern my life and works.

TIM HEATON

Hildegard of Bingen

Introducing Hildegard of Bingen needs more than words. Centuries before the term 'multimedia' was invented, Hildegard was using words, music and painting to put across her messages. If you can listen to her music and look at the illuminations in the next fortnight, it will enrich your encounter with this extraordinary woman.

Hildegard was born at the very end of the eleventh century, probably in 1098, and lived in what is now the western part of Germany, the Rhineland. Europe was recovering from a period of instability and expanding in different dimensions. Crusader armies were pushing south and east; new towns were springing up; new religious orders and new universities were being founded and a building boom was creating cathedrals, castles and civic buildings. Hildegard reflects this sense of expansion and new possibility in her wide-ranging interests and connections.

Power was divided, not always peacefully, between the state and the church. The leaders of both often came from the same aristocratic families, but were frequently at odds. The leaders of religious communities, abbots and abbesses, were powerful figures in their own right, though often beholden to wealthy families who gave them land and goods. Bishops and popes had their own armies, used to defend their titles and property. Germany was a patchwork of territories, ruled by dukes, margraves and counts, often at war with one another and with the king. But it was, at the same time, a highly hierarchical society, in which everyone knew their place, with God at the top of the pyramid.

Conflict extended to the top of the church; during Hildegard's lifetime twelve popes and ten antipopes were elected, and German kings and emperors often supported the unofficial antipopes against the pope. Hildegard was not afraid to get involved in this complex world, working for interdependence between church and state, with a proper division of their responsibilities. Hildegard has been venerated as a holy woman for many centuries, especially in Germany, but was not officially recognised as a saint by the Catholic Church until 2012, when the Pope declared her a Doctor of the Church, one of a very few women to be so recognised. I hope you will enjoy your encounter with this unique woman.

HELEN JULIAN CSF

A capable woman

A capable wife who can find? She is far more precious than jewels… She considers a field and buys it; with the fruit of her hands she plants a vineyard. She girds herself with strength, and makes her arms strong… She opens her hand to the poor, and reaches out her hands to the needy… Strength and dignity are her clothing, and she laughs at the time to come. She opens her mouth with wisdom, and the teaching of kindness is on her tongue.

Wife (capable or otherwise) is one of the few roles that Hildegard did not play during her long life, but she was certainly capable of multitasking, like the wife in Proverbs, and the range of her activities is quite dizzying. She had an unusually long life for her time, dying at the age of 81 in 1179, and she seems never to have stopped exploring new avenues.

She lived the religious life from the age of eight, presiding over an expanding community and then moving to a new location in search of greater independence. Later she founded a second community, which she visited regularly. Both attracted many members, especially from the aristocracy.

Hildegard was a prolific writer, drawing on the visions she experienced to write several books of theology. Although the illuminations that accompany them were probably not painted by her, she certainly supervised their production. Her knowledge of medicine, a common skill for nuns of her time, led to two books on natural history and medicine. She wrote music for her nuns to sing in worship, a biography of a local saint and commentaries on the Bible. She also engaged with the world outside her convent, writing to rulers in church and state to encourage or admonish them. She seems to have been unafraid of powerful people. At the age of 60, she set out on the first of four preaching tours, which took her to many parts of Germany, preaching for the reform of the church. The last of these tours took place when she was in her early 70s.

Do you have gifts you have not yet used? What prevents you from exploring them? Could Hildegard's example be an inspiration for you, no matter what your age?

HELEN JULIAN CSF

And the child was young

When [Hannah] had weaned [Samuel], she took him up with her, along with a three-year-old bull, an ephah of flour, and a skin of wine. She brought him to the house of the Lord at Shiloh; and the child was young. Then they slaughtered the bull, and they brought the child to Eli. And she said, 'Oh, my lord! As you live, my lord, I am the woman who was standing here in your presence, praying to the Lord. For this child I prayed; and the Lord has granted me the petition that I made to him. Therefore I have lent him to the Lord; as long as he lives, he is given to the Lord.'

The story of Samuel shows that offering a child to God has a long history. Hildegard was only eight when her parents dedicated her to God. Traditionally she is said to have been the tenth (and final) child, and could therefore be seen as a 'tithe' offering. Faith was important to the family; two of her brothers became priests, and a sister later joined Hildegard in her convent.

This offering may have been simply an act of devotion, but it may also have reflected the unusual nature of the child from an early age. She seems to have experienced visions from before she could speak, and perhaps it was in recognition of this gift that she left home so early. She was given into the care of a young noblewoman called Jutta, only six or seven years older than Hildegard herself. Jutta was already living an enclosed solitary life alongside the new Benedictine abbey of Disibodenberg; Hildegard may have joined her there or have lived with Jutta's family, instructed by an older woman called Uta who was also Jutta's mentor. But the course of her life was certainly set from an early age.

In any case, we know that when Hildegard was 15 she took the habit of a Benedictine nun and was part of the growing community around Jutta. When Jutta died in 1136, Hildegard became leader of an expanding community.

Think back to your earliest memory of God. Was your family supportive of your faith journey, or baffled, or hostile? Has your journey continued in the same direction, or has it changed, subtly or dramatically?

HELEN JULIAN CSF

Friendship: pleasures and pains

So [Naomi] said, 'See, your sister-in-law has gone back to her people and to her gods; return after your sister-in-law.' But Ruth said, 'Do not press me to leave you or to turn back from following you! Where you go, I will go; where you lodge, I will lodge; your people shall be my people, and your God my God. Where you die, I will die—there will I be buried. May the Lord do thus and so to me, and more as well, if even death parts me from you!' When Naomi saw that she was determined to go with her, she said no more to her.

Life within a religious community could be intense. In Hildegard's time, nuns were largely confined to their convent or abbey (Hildegard's later preaching tours were highly unusual), and depended on one another for friendship and support. This was not seen as a problem; both Aelred of Rievaulx and Bernard of Clairvaux wrote books on the importance of friendship in community life.

However, the friendship of Hildegard and one of her nuns, Richardis, does seem to have brought some difficulties. Richardis von Stade joined the community at Disibodenberg and worked closely with Hildegard, acting as one of her secretaries. Soon after the move to Rupertsberg, Richardis, who came from a very well-connected family, was elected as abbess of Bassum, in her brother's diocese. By now she was probably in her early 30s, ready to move out of Hildegard's shadow and into a position of responsibility. However, Hildegard was horrified by the prospect of losing Richardis and began a campaign to block the appointment, writing to her mother, to the Archbishop of Mainz, and even to the Pope. She claimed that she was concerned only for Richardis' well-being, but the tone of the letters rather belies this. Finally she turned to Richardis' brother, asking him to persuade Richardis to return. He seems to have had some success, but sadly Richardis died before the return took place. The episode shows Hildegard as a woman of strong emotions and perhaps gives a more human picture of her than we often see.

Reflect on your own history of friendship.
What have been the gifts and the difficulties?

HELEN JULIAN CSF

Radical or conservative?

But I want you to understand that Christ is the head of every man, and the husband is the head of his wife, and God is the head of Christ… Indeed, man was not made from woman, but woman from man. Neither was man created for the sake of woman, but woman for the sake of man. For this reason a woman ought to have a symbol of authority on her head, because of the angels. Nevertheless, in the Lord woman is not independent of man or man independent of woman. For just as woman came from man, so man comes through woman; but all things come from God.

Hildegard has been claimed by some as a feminist before her time—a radical, even revolutionary thinker. While some of what she did was certainly radical for a woman, much of what she wrote is more of her time. As is so often the case, the truth is complex.

Hildegard describes herself as a 'weak woman' and held some quite traditional views of gender relations. Women (she believed) were frailer than men, more passive and more diffuse in their energies. When she wrote about the four temperaments of women, she did so in terms of how they affected relationships with men, fertility and reproductive health. These elements were what constituted a woman's life. She described her times as an 'effeminate age' and this was not intended as a compliment! However, in her visions she saw the church, the synagogue and the virtues as female figures, and certainly not weak ones. She even had a vision of pure knowledge as a female figure dressed in a bishop's pallium.

She interpreted 1 Corinthians 11:9, 'Neither was man created for the sake of woman, but woman for the sake of man', in a way that stressed the complementarity of the sexes, both equally needed to produce offspring, who are themselves both female and male. And when she wrote about Proverbs 31:10–11, she described strength and weakness as common to both men and women, though expressed in different ways.

How do you make sense of the biblical texts on gender relations?
Are some no longer usable, or can they be reinterpreted
in the light of present scientific and psychological knowledge?

HELEN JULIAN CSF

Visions from God

About noon the next day, as they were on their journey and approaching the city, Peter went up on the roof to pray. He became hungry and wanted something to eat; and while it was being prepared, he fell into a trance. He saw the heaven opened and something like a large sheet coming down, being lowered to the ground by its four corners. In it were all kinds of four-footed creatures and reptiles and birds of the air. Then he heard a voice saying, 'Get up, Peter; kill and eat.'

Hildegard's age, like so many, saw women as secondary, and certainly not called to leadership in the wider church, so how could women claim authority for their words? One of the few ways available to them was through visions. There was a long tradition of visions being given to all sorts of people, and as messages from God they could not easily be ignored.

Hildegard, as we've seen, received visions from a very early age. However, for much of her life she mentioned them only to a few close friends, until, in her early 40s, she received a command from God to share what she saw and heard, and began to write her first book. Even then she was reticent, and six years later she was writing to Bernard of Clairvaux to ask for his validation of her visions, which he gave. Around the same time, the Pope read her book and authorised her to continue her work. By this time she was nearly 50.

We may well be curious about how Hildegard received her visions, and so were her contemporaries. In response to their questions she recounted how she saw a light, not like an ordinary light, which produced images, and sometimes heard a voice addressing her in Latin. This happened in full consciousness, not in a dream or a trance, not with physical eyes and ears, but with the inner eyes and ears.

How do you receive God's teaching? It may be through reading the Bible, conversations with friends, dreams or prayer of many sorts. Have you ever received something you would describe as a vision and, if so, have you had the confidence to share it with anyone else?

HELEN JULIAN CSF

Authority and action

'Who is like you, O Lord, among the gods? Who is like you, majestic in
holiness, awesome in splendour, doing wonders?... In your steadfast
love you led the people whom you redeemed; you guided them by your
strength to your holy abode... You brought them in and planted them
on the mountain of your own possession, the place, O Lord, that you
made your abode, the sanctuary, O Lord, that your hands have
established. The Lord will reign for ever and ever.'

Visions gave Hildegard a certain authority but she still struggled to exercise this authority in daily life. As her community grew, the restrictions of
being dependent on the monks of Disibodenberg became more difficult.
They had insufficient space and were financially dependent. In a vision,
Hildegard was told to leave Disibodenberg with her sisters and to found a
separate community. The monks did not easily agree; they would lose the
dowries of the sisters and the kudos of having many well-connected
women living alongside their monastery. However, after Hildegard took to
her bed and could not physically be moved, the abbot agreed that her
desire was of God, and in 1150 Hildegard and 20 sisters moved a day's
journey down the River Nahe to Rupertsberg, where a new convent had
been built. Financial autonomy took until 1158 to achieve, and the early
years were ones of poverty and hardship.

Another kind of hardship struck the community near the end of
Hildegard's life, with another clash of authority. She allowed a nobleman,
who had been excommunicated but then reconciled with the church, to
be buried in the convent cemetery. The church authorities seem not to
have believed in his reconciliation, and they imposed an interdict on the
community. This meant that the sisters could neither receive the sacraments nor sing the Divine Office—two key parts of their life. It was the last
year of Hildegard's life, and the prospect of dying without the sacraments
would have been terrifying to her. She appealed to the Archbishop of
Mainz, who finally lifted the interdict. Six months later Hildegard died.

---

*Have you ever needed to stand up to faith leaders to do what you believed
God was calling you to? What resources helped you in that struggle?*

HELEN JULIAN CSF

Gifts of healing

Honour physicians for their services, for the Lord created them; for their gift of healing comes from the Most High, and they are rewarded by the king. The skill of physicians makes them distinguished, and in the presence of the great they are admired. The Lord created medicines out of the earth, and the sensible will not despise them. Was not water made sweet with a tree in order that its power might be known? And he gave skill to human beings that he might be glorified in his marvellous works.

The visions that played an important part in Hildegard's life were often linked with illness. The vision that led to her finally sharing these words and images from God with the world itself came at a time of prolonged illness, and a number of other key events in her life were preceded by similar experiences. Medical historians have speculated (from studying the paintings of her visions) that she suffered from severe migraine, but of course there's no way of being sure.

However, it is likely that her own illnesses led to a particular interest in medicine. As we can see from the passage above, as well as other Old and New Testament passages, healing in all its forms was seen as a gift from God, and Hildegard would not have considered her more scientific books as materially different from the theological works in this respect. Women in general and nuns in particular were seen as being skilled in medical matters, with knowledge of the healing powers of plants—and Hildegard also wrote of less easily available substances, such as parts of ostriches, whales, vultures, lions and leopards. Her interest in healing extended to those suffering from mental illness, in particular a young woman called Sigewize, who then joined her community.

Hildegard's two books dealing with medicine also cover natural history; one lists almost 1000 plants and animals, describing their habitats, edibility and medicinal uses. These books come from the earlier part of her life, before her public ministry began, and show us a curious and attentive woman, gathering and ordering information about the world.

---

*God of healing, may we honour the world you have created
and use it wisely for our own and others' good.*

HELEN JULIAN CSF

Preaching God's word

And the spirits of prophets are subject to the prophets, for God is a God not of disorder but of peace. (As in all the churches of the saints, women should be silent in the churches. For they are not permitted to speak, but should be subordinate, as the law also says. If there is anything they desire to know, let them ask their husbands at home. For it is shameful for a woman to speak in church. Or did the word of God originate with you? Or are you the only ones it has reached?)

Silence was not one of Hildegard's most notable qualities. Words poured out of her once she began to share her visions, and she would undoubtedly have spoken regularly to her own community of sisters as their leader, teaching and admonishing them.

In an even more unusual move, in her early 60s, she embarked on the first of four preaching tours, travelling from her monastery to various parts of Germany. The first three took place in this period. Then, after a gap of some years, during which she founded a second community, also under her leadership, she made a final tour in her early 70s. Two of her tours followed periods of sickness, in which she believed she was commissioned to share God's word. There is little concrete information about how she travelled or where she preached, although she undoubtedly spoke both in monasteries and in churches. Hence, she was a woman preaching to men, a very unusual activity for her time; indeed, it was unusual for a nun to leave her convent at all.

What did she preach? Some of her sermons were written down and circulated, and from these we can see that her main concern was to call the clergy back to their true calling and away from worldly power and wealth. She also preached fiercely against some of the heretical sects that were active in Germany, especially the Cathars. They held that the material world was entirely evil and that only the spiritual was pure and praiseworthy. Hildegard's concern was for the well-being of the church, which was threatened by heresy.

If you could preach just one sermon, where would you choose to do it and what would you say?

HELEN JULIAN CSF

Speaking truth to power

For Herod had arrested John, bound him, and put him in prison on account of Herodias, his brother Philip's wife, because John had been telling him, 'It is not lawful for you to have her.' Though Herod wanted to put him to death, he feared the crowd, because they regarded him as a prophet. But when Herod's birthday came, the daughter of Herodias danced before the company, and she pleased Herod so much that he promised on oath to grant her whatever she might ask. Prompted by her mother, she said, 'Give me the head of John the Baptist here on a platter.'

It was not only in preaching that Hildegard spoke to the powerful people of her day. She also wrote letters to rulers in both church and state, in her own country and further afield—and these were not simply courteous assurances of prayer. We can see this in her letters to Emperor Frederick I (Frederick Barbarossa), king of Germany from 1152 to 1190. Her first letter congratulates him on his election, sets before him an exalted view of leadership, and asks God's blessing on him. More than a decade later, after Frederick had supported the antipope Victor IV, Hildegard wrote to rebuke him implicitly for this move, and to remind him that as a 'servant of God' he should use his power for more than his own ambitions. But she also promised to pray that the emperor and his second wife would have the son they longed for—and they soon had not one but two sons.

When the antipope died, however, Frederick was instrumental in the election of a second, Paschalis III. Hildegard wrote a short and curt letter, accusing him of behaving childishly and warning that he was in danger of losing the grace of God in his life. Finally, in 1168, when a third antipope was elected with Frederick's support, Hildegard sent a letter consisting entirely of biblical texts on divine retribution for the wicked.

This was perhaps a dangerous move on Hildegard's part; prophets' lives often end unhappily in scripture. But she had a strong sense of responsibility for her world and would not stay silent.

God of the prophets, give me courage to speak out
when you give me the words.

HELEN JULIAN CSF

Singing a new song

Rejoice in the Lord, O you righteous. Praise befits the upright. Praise the Lord with the lyre; make melody to him with the harp of ten strings. Sing to him a new song; play skilfully on the strings, with loud shouts… Let all the earth fear the Lord; let all the inhabitants of the world stand in awe of him. For he spoke, and it came to be; he commanded, and it stood firm.

It is perhaps through her music that many people first encounter Hildegard, but it was only around the 800th anniversary of her birth that her music began to be performed again after centuries of silence. The body of her surviving work is greater than for many other medieval composers; there is a morality play, and nearly 80 other compositions. Once again, Hildegard ascribes these works to divine inspiration, asserting that she received both words and melody in her visions, though she had no musical training. Most of her music seems to have been written in the 1140s and collected in the 1150s; and it was, of course, written almost exclusively for use in worship, in daily prayer and praise by the nuns of her community.

The sisters would have gathered several times every day in their chapel to sing the psalms, to hear the Bible read and to celebrate the feasts and seasons of the church year. Much of Hildegard's music was written for these feasts and seasons, in celebration of the Virgin Mary, of the confessors and martyrs, of God the Father and of the Holy Spirit.

Hildegard saw music as far more than just a pleasant interlude in worship; it was a way for God's creation to echo back to him joy and thanks, returning to the unity with God for which it was created. She held that Adam had been created to sing with the angels and, in singing, all of God's people could glimpse that sweetness and delight. No wonder music was such a crucial part of daily life in Hildegard's community.

How does music feature in your worship and praise of God?
What 'new song' might you sing to God to express your joy
and thanks to God for his creation?

HELEN JULIAN CSF

Devising artistic designs

Then Moses said to the Israelites: See, the Lord has called by name Bezalel son of Uri son of Hur, of the tribe of Judah; he has filled him with divine spirit, with skill, intelligence, and knowledge in every kind of craft, to devise artistic designs, to work in gold, silver, and bronze, in cutting stones for setting, and in carving wood, in every kind of craft... He has filled [him] with skill to do every kind of work done by an artisan or by a designer or by an embroiderer in blue, purple, and crimson yarns, and in fine linen, or by a weaver—by any sort of artisan or skilled designer.

As well as many words and much music, Hildegard is credited with the illuminations that illustrate some of her books, especially those recounting her visions. As she used secretaries to write the books, it is likely that artists—perhaps her sisters or some of the monks of Disibodenberg—actually created these wonderful glowing paintings. But it's generally accepted that Hildegard was the controlling mind, not least because they do not just illustrate her visions but provide a new layer of meaning. It seems unlikely that Hildegard, with her high regard for the visions, would have allowed someone else to alter their meaning.

If possible, do find a way of seeing some of these illuminations; they are striking and sometimes quite disturbing, almost hallucinatory. It's been suggested that they support the thesis that Hildegard suffered from migraine, and that the visual disturbance characteristic of migraine is reflected in the paintings. The visionary quality is strong in these paintings, which often have their own take on the subject. For example, in a picture of creation and fall, Eve is shown being born out of Adam's side as a white cloud. The cloud contains many stars, which represent the human race. In another painting, the universe is shown as an egg shape, with the four elements of earth, air, fire and water at the centre. The sun represents Christ, and the moon the church. Here, stars represent acts of piety, and the whole egg is embraced by a circle of fire—God's love.

How do you use your creativity? You may need to collaborate with someone else to bring your 'vision' to life.

HELEN JULIAN CSF

God's green world

Then God said, 'Let the earth put forth vegetation: plants yielding seed, and fruit trees of every kind on earth that bear fruit with the seed in it.' And it was so. The earth brought forth vegetation: plants yielding seed of every kind, and trees of every kind bearing fruit with the seed in it. And God saw that it was good. And there was evening and there was morning, the third day.

'Viriditas' is a word that Hildegard uses often, and it is central to her thought. Its literal translation is 'greenness', but it can also mean freshness, vitality, fertility, fecundity, fruitfulness or growth. It carries a sense of spring and new life, and in Hildegard's writings it has, in particular, a deep sense of health on all levels—spiritual, moral and physical. She uses it to refer to a desirable quality of order and harmony, which draws on the life within the earth, especially in the form of moisture. The Rhineland, where Hildegard lived, is a very fertile and green land, and this must have influenced the images she uses.

Greenness, for Hildegard, is not a static quality but a power at work: 'The rivers give rise to smaller streams that sustain the earth by their greening power' (*Book of Divine Works*). In the spiritual realm, the Holy Spirit is the giver of life, pouring out green freshness into human hearts. Christ is the living vine: those who drink from him in the Eucharist become green and fruitful, bringing forth good fruit. Throughout the Middle Ages, Christ was traditionally pictured with green eyes.

As viriditas gives life, so a loss of greenness and moisture is, for Hildegard, a sign of lack of health and harmony, even of sin. In paradise everything was green and flourishing, but Hildegard describes the church of her own day as dried up, lacking in moisture and therefore weak and ineffective.

Reflect on what enables God's 'greening' life to flow through you. How do you make and sustain contact with the deepest source of life and flourishing? Can you identify what might block this life— what might make you feel dried up, disordered and out of harmony with the world around you?

HELEN JULIAN CSF

Lady Wisdom

**Does not wisdom call, and does not understanding raise her voice?...
The Lord created me at the beginning of his work, the first of his acts of
long ago. Ages ago I was set up, at the first, before the beginning of the
earth. When there were no depths I was brought forth, when there were
no springs abounding with water. Before the mountains had been
shaped, before the hills, I was brought forth.**

'Greenness' is one of Hildegard's theological ideas that resonates today.
Another is her emphasis on Wisdom, a female figure who, in Hildegard's
theology, was present from the beginning of the world and cooperated
with God in the creation of everything in the cosmos. 'Wisdom' is a feminine word in Hebrew, Greek and Latin; more importantly, she is a feminine
figure wherever she appears in the Old Testament. The first of these
appearances is in Proverbs, and then she reappears in the Apocryphal
books of Ecclesiasticus and The Wisdom of Solomon.

Hildegard encountered Wisdom in her visions and drew out the meaning of each detail. In her written description of one of her visions,
Hildegard describes Wisdom as a figure of great beauty, who is joined to
God the Father in a dance, and protects the people of the earth. Her head
shines like lightning, both drawing the eye and being too bright to look
upon, as God is both terrible and enticing. Her feet cannot be seen, for
only God can see her way and know her secrets. She is splendidly dressed
in a golden tunic, and a long belt studded with precious jewels extends to
her feet, symbolising the idea that her way extends to the end of the world
and is adorned with God's holy commands.

It all sounds far beyond us mere humans, but in a later book Hildegard
wrote that we, God's human creation, can become Wisdom's robe when
we follow God's commandments—and, in a link to 'viriditas', this robe is
green. Wisdom, through her role in creation and her loving challenges,
draws us into the cosmic struggle of good and evil and leads us toward
redemption.

---

*Lord, may divine wisdom guide me along the way that leads to life;
please show me her splendour.*

HELEN JULIAN CSF

Everything belongs together

In the day that the Lord God made the earth and the heavens, when no plant of the field was yet in the earth and no herb of the field had yet sprung up—for the Lord God had not caused it to rain upon the earth, and there was no one to till the ground… then the Lord God formed man from the dust of the ground, and breathed into his nostrils the breath of life; and the man became a living being.

Hildegard is difficult to sum up. In some respects she seems very modern, in others very much of her time. On one hand, she is scathing about the state of the church in her day, deeply conservative in her desire for reform. On the other hand, her visions and illuminations take her at times into uncharted theological territory, and her image of 'greenness' resonates with our present ecological concerns.

Perhaps one of her illuminations can provide a way in. It shows God at the top of the picture, with Christ immediately below. Christ's immensely long arms are embracing a flaming wheel, inside of which are oceans, winds and animals—and he is forcing it into motion. At the heart of the wheel is a human figure, naked and unashamed; and in the lower left corner, we see Hildegard herself recording her vision. Humanity and the rest of creation (and, hence, the Creator) are inextricably linked, and God's life flows through all that he has made. But humanity has a special role within this creation because we possess reason, and so we can choose to cooperate with God's goodness or to defy him. Even more than that, creation itself is marked with a human outline, and humanity contains elements of the universe within itself—that is, humanity is a microcosm of the world's macrocosm. Both are intrinsically good, made by God in love, capable of failure and of sin but also capable of cooperating with one another and with God.

There is so much more! As we end our time with Hildegard, take a moment to reflect on what you have learnt and what you might want to explore further—perhaps theology, music or art. Give thanks to God for Hildegard's life and commit yourself again to God's service, as she did.

HELEN JULIAN CSF

Moses: wilderness pioneer

In the next two weeks we shall be in the company of Moses, and we join him just after the sensational crossing of the Red Sea as he embarks on his journey through the desert. As he left the lush pasturelands around the Egyptian Nile, little did he imagine that he would never dwell amid such fertility again. After the parting of the great waters, he and his people were at last free, and they were on their way to the promised land. Yet the journey to that blessed place was a protracted and arduous plod through an arid and dusty land. Hardly had the spray of the Red Sea dried on the robes of the tribes of Israel before there were complaints, doubts, fears and strife in abundance. Moses had to face the rough terrains of both the land and the human soul. Hardly a day went by for him without having to deal with some crisis or other—but in the wilderness days there were also great high points that sustained this extraordinary and faithful leader.

When the adventures of Moses came to be written up, they filled several books. We can't do justice to his life and witness in just two weeks of Bible notes, but we shall visit a handful of stories that tell us much about this man and his rugged commitment to a mysterious yet wonderful God. The God who had caught his attention through a blazing bush on the slopes of Horeb was with him every inch of the desert way. We can imagine the intensity of the thrill that ran through his whole being on the day when he saw in the distance the beautiful and fertile land that was to be his and his people's destiny. And yet, because of what may seem to us a fairly minor offence, he was never allowed to set foot in that land of promise.

Nevertheless, the journey was forming something deep in him and his people, for Moses was a pioneer of the spirit and, through his devotion to the 'I am' God, he caught sight of a world that was even more beautiful than the lush pastures of fair Canaan.

MICHAEL MITTON

Listening in the desert

There the Lord made for them a statute and an ordinance and there he put them to the test. He said, 'If you will listen carefully to the voice of the Lord your God, and do what is right in his sight, and give heed to his commandments and keep all his statutes, I will not bring upon you any of the diseases that I brought upon the Egyptians; for I am the Lord who heals you.'

Once Miriam had packed up her tambourine and dancing shoes, the great company of the children of Israel set off to the north of the Sinai Peninsula to begin their journey to the promised land. No doubt, many in the company supposed that the journey would be neither long nor arduous, so it came as a shock to find that, three days in, they were faced with a major crisis—a serious lack of water. At a place called Marah, they were thrilled to discover a plentiful supply of flowing water, only to find that it was undrinkable. Their first response was to grumble, and a deputation marched up to Moses. Through their dry lips they told him what they thought of his organisation and route-planning skills. This was to be a repeated pattern of complaint and it nearly exasperated Moses.

On this occasion, Moses, fairly parched himself, cries out to the Lord and listens for instructions. He is shown a piece of wood, which turns out to have God-blessed power to turn foul water into good. We are told that God 'put them to the test'—finding out what they were made of. Three days in, and they have an ideal opportunity to exercise their faith muscles. To develop such muscles, they have to learn to listen. It is a major lesson for any wilderness journey: when the situation is testing, stop and listen to God. He will have provided something—maybe as ordinary as an old wooden stick, but in the hand of faith it becomes the very thing that opens a stream of life.

Lord, when my pathway leads me to desert places, remind me to pause and to listen, and to find the gift that leads me to a stream of living water.

MICHAEL MITTON

Losing the mentality of the slave

The whole congregation of the Israelites complained against Moses and Aaron in the wilderness. The Israelites said to them, 'If only we had died by the hand of the Lord in the land of Egypt, when we sat by the fleshpots and ate our fill of bread; for you have brought us out into this wilderness to kill this whole assembly with hunger.' Then the Lord said to Moses, 'I am going to rain bread from heaven for you, and each day the people shall go out and gather enough for that day.'

Six weeks into the journey, there is another crisis. This time it is not about water but about food. The sound of grumbling stomachs is quickly drowned by the sound of grumbling voices. The entire company let Moses know that they are not happy. They do what we often do, once we get into our stride of grumbling: we idealise a far-from-ideal past. Many a church leader has been faced with complaints couched in testimonies of a glorious past that plainly never existed. The children of Israel have neatly forgotten the days of severe slavery and forced labour—but it is the mentality of the slave that is at work here. They imagine both Moses and God to be severe taskmasters who will stretch the people to their very limits to get out of them what they need. The journey in the wilderness is an opportunity to learn that they are not slaves but children. Slaves presume hostility and hardship; beloved children presume care and protection.

So the heavenly Father pours out miraculous manna from heaven and adds meat to the diet in the form of quails. When we hit our own desert experiences, it is remarkably easy to default to the mentality of the slave. We imagine that others are being treated better than we are; we exaggerate the blessings of the past to reinforce our plight in the present time; in our minds we turn ministers, bosses and friends into slave-drivers. Moses invites us into the new mindset of the beloved child who knows that the good things of God are never far away.

Father, when I tread the desert path,
remind me that I journey as a child of God.

MICHAEL MITTON

Where the battle is won

Then Amalek came and fought with Israel at Rephidim. Moses said to Joshua, 'Choose some men for us and go out; fight with Amalek. Tomorrow I will stand on the top of the hill with the staff of God in my hand.' So Joshua did as Moses told him, and fought with Amalek, while Moses, Aaron, and Hur went up to the top of the hill. Whenever Moses held up his hand, Israel prevailed; and whenever he lowered his hand, Amalek prevailed.

As if there wasn't enough trouble happening in his own camp, Moses has to face a new threat. This time it is from an army from Amalek, who see their opportunity to attack this travelling tribe. The story introduces us to a new hero, Joshua, and he has the task of leading a troop of fighters against the marauding aggressors. Moses is clear about the battle strategy: while Joshua fights in the valley, he will ascend the hill and look down upon the battle. His job will be that of the intercessor.

The battle gets underway and Moses takes his station on the hillside, supported by Aaron and Hur. It quickly becomes evident that the fate of the battle will be determined by the elevation of Moses' hands. Moses is learning that the journey of faith with God does not mean the absence of trouble. There are battles in the valleys of this world, but Moses is finding out about the authority and power of God released through persistent prayer. He is the forerunner of the prayer warriors and prophets who step back from the battle zone and call down from heaven the blessings of God. Such a vantage point gives sightings of the plans of God and the enemy.

Years later, Jesus told his disciples that there would be plenty of tribulations in this world. He does not shield us from the troubles, but when the children of God know the authority of Christ, they can be of good cheer, for he has won the battle (see John 16:33).

When troubles come my way, O Lord, lead me to the high place
where I can know your power and authority.

MICHAEL MITTON

The gift of the practical mind

[Jethro said] 'If you do this, and God so commands you, then you will be able to endure, and all these people will go to their home in peace.' So Moses listened to his father-in-law and did all that he had said. Moses chose able men from all Israel and appointed them as heads over the people, as officers over thousands, hundreds, fifties, and tens. And they judged the people at all times; hard cases they brought to Moses, but any minor case they decided themselves. Then Moses let his father-in-law depart, and he went off to his own country.

It was just before the episode with the burning bush when Moses met Jethro, a priest in the land of Midian. He was also called Reuel, meaning 'friend of God' (Exodus 2:18). Moses married Jethro's daughter Zipporah and stayed with him for many years before his epic flight from Egypt.

Jethro has clearly been keeping up with the news of his son-in-law and, in Exodus 18, he is thrilled to hear of the way God has led Moses. This friend of God recognises the workings of his Lord in this remarkable journey. It must have been wonderful for Moses to be in the company of such a faith-filled father-in-law. Rather than complaining about bitter water and lack of bread, Jethro sees the signs of God's grace in the wilderness. In many ways he is a kindred spirit with Moses.

But lest we should think they spent their whole time in a spiritual prayer and praise meeting, the story reveals that Jethro was a very practical strategist and leader, with much to teach Moses. He carefully watches his son-in-law getting exhausted with a style of leadership that holds the reins too tightly. Moses must learn to share his leadership with others. Jethro sees gifts in others and helps Moses to trust those gifts. One of the lessons of the wilderness is about discovering our need of others. It is a time to be on the lookout for a faith-filled friend of God who brings a different perspective, to lighten our load.

In my times of weariness, lead me, Lord, to a friend of faith,
and let me learn from them.

MICHAEL MITTON

The thick darkness of God

When all the people witnessed the thunder and lightning, the sound of the trumpet, and the mountain smoking, they were afraid and trembled and stood at a distance, and said to Moses, 'You speak to us, and we will listen; but do not let God speak to us, or we will die.' Moses said to the people, 'Do not be afraid; for God has come only to test you and to put the fear of him upon you so that you do not sin.' Then the people stood at a distance, while Moses drew near to the thick darkness where God was.

Moses leads the people to Mt Sinai, and it becomes clear that this is such a holy mountain that only Moses may go near it (Exodus 19). Moses is allowed to ascend the mountain to meet with God, and there he receives the commandments by which the people are to conduct their lives. As God delivers them, the people wait in the valley and are terrified to witness a spectacular thunderstorm on the mountain. This is not a God they want to allow too close: they would sooner get the message from the less frightening Moses.

In today's passage we have an intriguing reference to Moses drawing near to the 'thick darkness where God was'. The cloud over the mountain was so dense that it was like deep darkness. The people marvelled that Moses had the courage to step right into it, but Moses was learning about the God who was leading them. For a start, he could see that the thunder and lightning were there to evoke not cringing terror, but wonder and delight at God's power. He was also learning that there was a darkness about God, which was a darkness not of dread but of intimacy. Moses was being invited into a secret place for a one-to-one with his Maker, and in conversation with God he learned extraordinary wisdom.

Centuries later, Moses was allowed to visit another mountain, covered with dense cloud, where he met with the transfigured Jesus (Matthew 17:1–8), whose work was to make it possible for all humans to enter holy ground and converse intimately with their Maker.

What does the darkness of God mean to you?

MICHAEL MITTON

Changing the mind of God

But Moses implored the Lord his God, and said, 'O Lord, why does your wrath burn hot against your people, whom you brought out of the land of Egypt with great power and with a mighty hand?... Turn from your fierce wrath; change your mind and do not bring disaster on your people. Remember Abraham, Isaac, and Israel, your servants, how you swore to them by your own self, saying to them, "I will multiply your descendants like the stars of heaven, and all this land that I have promised I will give to your descendants, and they shall inherit it for ever."' And the Lord changed his mind about the disaster that he planned to bring on his people.

Today's passage comes after the terrible episode in which the people constructed a makeshift god out of their golden earrings, when they feared that Moses had disappeared for ever up the holy mountain. The pattern by which people prefer gold to God is age-old. Moses' summit with the Lord is brought to an abrupt halt as God notices the rebellion in the valley. The divine sentence for such a crime is the elimination of the people. Witnessing the anger of God must have been a terrible thing, but Moses does not flinch and stands his ground. He is not willing to give up his people without a fight, despite their waywardness.

So in today's passage we see him reasoning with God and calling on him to remember the oaths he swore to the earlier patriarchs. It is an incredibly audacious thing to do: what right has he, a sinful mortal, to try to change the mind of Almighty God? The answer has to be in the fact that Moses has learned to dwell with God in his darkness. In the darkness of intimate friendship, he has learned that he is safe, no matter what, even if he should challenge God's ways. In this safe place he makes his appeal. He is a man of hope, for he can see that the people, though rebellious, can still fulfil the purposes of God. Such levels of faith and hope always touch the heart of God.

What issues do you want to bring to God in the intimacy of darkness?

MICHAEL MITTON

Yearning for the glory of God

Moses said, 'Show me your glory, I pray.' And he said, 'I will make all my goodness pass before you, and will proclaim before you the name, 'The Lord'; and I will be gracious to whom I will be gracious, and will show mercy on whom I will show mercy. But', he said, 'you cannot see my face; for no one shall see me and live.' And the Lord continued, 'See, there is a place by me where you shall stand on the rock; and while my glory passes by I will put you in a cleft of the rock.'

Moses has established a special tent for meeting with God (Exodus 33:7–11), which becomes a powerful place of encounter with God, similar to Mt Sinai. Moses was often found in this holy place and he clearly enjoyed many conversations with God, but their companionship began to evoke a new yearning within the heart of Moses. When he met with God, there was always much business to discuss, yet this was not going to be enough for him. For Moses, religion was not simply about following a complex rule-book and behaving himself. It was primarily about getting to know this wonderful God who delighted to live among his people. So there comes a time when Moses daringly says words to the effect of, 'I don't just want to know your ways; I want to know *you*.' His longing is to see God in all his glory.

God agrees but knows that it is too much for Moses to see his face, so, while he does reveal his glory to Moses, he also shelters him from an encounter that would overpower him. We get the sense that this glimpse of the glory of God gives Moses such a fiery and lasting vision that not even his failure to enter the promised land could quench it. It should not surprise us that, when Jesus was revealed in his glory on the mount of transfiguration, Moses was there. If the choice was between seeing the glory of God or dwelling in Canaan, Moses would have gone for the glory any day.

Lord, when I get too occupied with doing the works of God,
stir in me a Moses-like longing for your glory.

MICHAEL MITTON

The heart of a humble prophet

Then the Lord came down in a pillar of cloud, and stood at the entrance of the tent, and called Aaron and Miriam; and they both came forward. And he said, 'Hear my words: When there are prophets among you, I the Lord make myself known to them in visions; I speak to them in dreams. Not so with my servant Moses; he is entrusted with all my house. With him I speak face to face—clearly, not in riddles; and he beholds the form of the Lord. Why then were you not afraid to speak against my servant Moses?'

Moses has become accustomed to the grumblings of the people but it must be especially galling when his own brother and sister grumble against him. Their particular gripe is that he has married a Cushite, but we get the impression that their complaint is motivated by jealousy. The writer tells us that one of Moses' qualities was humility (Numbers 12:3), which is one reason why he could draw so close to God. Aaron and Miriam are keen to find fault in their brother and, no doubt, are taken aback when the Lord comes down in a pillar of cloud and speaks to them. God tells them about the intimate friendship he enjoys with Moses, and that such a friendship should be respected by all. As a punishment for challenging Moses, Miriam is afflicted with leprosy, but once again the friend of God changes the divine mind and she is delivered.

The story gives us another insight into the character of Moses. At times it must have been very lonely for him, especially when even his nearest and dearest were attacking him, but he found a refuge in God. Moses was someone whom God could trust with his messages. Moses was not going to embellish or spoil them to use for his own ends. God could speak plainly to him. By this stage in the story we see that a deep and robust friendship has developed between Moses and God. Jesus called his disciples 'friends' (John 15:15): we are therefore his friends, and, like Moses, we are invited into this place of meeting.

What does it mean to you to be a friend of God?

MICHAEL MITTON

Voices of fear and faith

Moses sent them to spy out the land of Canaan, and said to them, 'Go up there into the Negeb, and go up into the hill country, and see what the land is like, and whether the people who live in it are strong or weak, whether they are few or many, and whether the land they live in is good or bad, and whether the towns that they live in are unwalled or fortified, and whether the land is rich or poor, and whether there are trees in it or not. Be bold, and bring some of the fruit of the land.'

We come now to a tantalising episode in Moses' life, in which some of the Israelites finally set foot in the land of their dreams. Moses chooses a leader from each tribe; they enter Canaan at the south and make an extensive 250-mile journey up to the north and back. Joshua, Caleb and the others return laden with delicious fruit from the fertile land. Such exotic food must have looked magnificent to Moses and the others waiting in the desert. Moses' heart no doubt skips a beat as he hears news of this lush and fertile land, now so close.

The mission team give their report, which includes some bad news. For ten members of the team, this bad news far outweighs the good, and they succeed in spreading fear in the camp. Caleb and Joshua try persuading the company to take the opportunity to enter the land, but they are shouted down. Numbers 14 is a dreadfully sad chapter in which God tells them that he would have gone with them, and they would have conquered their enemies and settled in the land. Once again, Moses manages to change the mind of God through his intercession, and the people are spared, but their rebellion means they must journey another 40 years in the wilderness. It is a sobering story about the way human nature too often listens to the voices of fear over the voices of faith. We have to learn to trust the Caleb and Joshua voices of faith that silence our inner voices of fear.

Lord, have mercy on my fears,
and grant me a heart that thrills
to the sounds of faith.

MICHAEL MITTON

The snake on the pole

Then the Lord sent poisonous serpents among the people, and they bit the people, so that many Israelites died. The people came to Moses and said, 'We have sinned by speaking against the Lord and against you; pray to the Lord to take away the serpents from us.' So Moses prayed for the people. And the Lord said to Moses, 'Make a poisonous serpent, and set it on a pole; and everyone who is bitten shall look at it and live.' So Moses made a serpent of bronze, and put it upon a pole; and whenever a serpent bit someone, that person would look at the serpent of bronze and live.

Today's story starts with yet another complaint against Moses, when he is offered the usual whinge that life was much better in Egypt so everyone should head back there (Numbers 21:4–5). It is in response to this that God sends poisonous snakes into the camp, which puts the fear of God back into the people. Once again Moses is found in intercession for his people: for all their annoying grumbles, he is still very much on their side and longs to protect them from the snakes. God hears his cry and offers a very strange solution to the problem. Moses is to make a bronze snake and set it on a pole. If anyone is bitten, they come to the pole and are freed from the effects of the poison.

But why not just get rid of the snakes? It seems that God is using this device to forge something new in the hearts of the people. Their natural inclination is to look at the problems of food shortage, snakes and so on, and complain to Moses. God is helping them to grow up in the life of faith so that, when problems come, their first instinct is to look to God rather than complain. By setting the serpent on a pole, God effectively says, 'Look, here is the threat, but I am greater than the threat. You have it in you to live by confidence in me.' God knows that life is full of threats but he loves to adjust our default response from complaint to trust.

What is your default response in the face of threats?

MICHAEL MITTON

The waters of Meribah

So Moses took the staff from before the Lord, as he had commanded him. Moses and Aaron gathered the assembly together before the rock, and he said to them, 'Listen, you rebels, shall we bring water for you out of this rock?' Then Moses lifted up his hand and struck the rock twice with his staff; water came out abundantly, and the congregation and their livestock drank. But the Lord said to Moses and Aaron, 'Because you did not trust in me, to show my holiness before the eyes of the Israelites, therefore you shall not bring this assembly into the land that I have given them.'

This story brings us towards the end of the 40 years of wandering. The Israelites are back at Kadesh, and the promised land is a whisker away. Even after all these years of journeying, with the new homeland within reach, there is still grumbling in the camp and vain longings to be back in Egypt. The specific complaint this time is the lack of water, so Moses and Aaron take it straight to God in the tent of meeting. The glory of the Lord descends, and God tells Moses to speak to the rock, and water shall flow. As Moses leaves the tent, something in him cracks: the years of the people's complaints have taken their toll and, rather than speaking to the rock, he shouts at the people and smashes his stick against the rock. There is water, but there is also a terrible rebuke from God, who tells Moses that for this misdemeanour he will not be entering the promised land.

There is no record of Moses' response, and we might expect him to be heartbroken. But by now Moses is so in tune with the will of God that the homing device in him is now not a piece of land, however full of significance. It is much more to do with the presence of God who has been wonderfully evident even in this desert wilderness. We get the sense that Moses is at peace, for his true destiny is the heart of God.

Lord, I have my longings, but grant me a Moses heart,
that my deep longing may be companionship with you.

MICHAEL MITTON

Sightings of mercy

The Lord will scatter you among the peoples; only a few of you will be left among the nations where the Lord will lead you… From there you will seek the Lord your God, and you will find him if you search after him with all your heart and soul. In your distress, when all these things have happened to you in time to come, you will return to the Lord your God and heed him. Because the Lord your God is a merciful God, he will neither abandon you nor destroy you; he will not forget the covenant with your ancestors that he swore to them.

The book of Deuteronomy is a sermon—probably the longest ever preached! It is Moses' last sermon, delivered on the plains of Moab before his final rest. Here Moses includes a summary of the lessons the people of God have learned during their long wilderness journey and a reminder of God's laws. Moses will send the people on their way, and by now he knows that they are capable of great courage and faith, but also great weakness and sinfulness. As he peers towards the lush lands of their hopes, he also spies into the long-distant future and glimpses the exile that will befall the people of God because of their disobedience. But his lessons in the wilderness have taught him much about the character of God who, above all things, is merciful.

These early books of the Bible include laws and punishments that, to our ears today, sound very severe. We cringe from modern-day stories of religious people of varying faiths meting out terrifying punishments in the name of God. We cannot hide from some of the disturbing stories in the life of Moses. In today's passage we see an elderly Moses squinting into the far distance and seeing humans failing yet again. But beyond all the failings and punishments, there is at the root of all things a merciful God. Maybe he was even catching sight of the Son of God who preached about a grace stronger than law, and whose life and death released an eternal wave of mercy into this world.

What does the mercy of God mean to you?

MICHAEL MITTON

God is with you

Then Moses summoned Joshua and said to him in the sight of all Israel: 'Be strong and bold, for you are the one who will go with this people into the land that the Lord has sworn to their ancestors to give them; and you will put them in possession of it. It is the Lord who goes before you. He will be with you; he will not fail you or forsake you. Do not fear or be dismayed.'

Moses has been a remarkable pioneer. As a Hebrew prince in the palace of Pharaoh, he heard the call of God to lead his people out of slavery back to the land promised to Abraham. He witnessed the plagues in Egypt and the miraculous parting of the waters. He led a huge company of people through barren wastelands for over 40 years, often getting nothing but complaints for his troubles. He followed the cloud and the fire, had extraordinary meetings with God in all his glory and heard from God about the laws that would be the foundation for the life of the people. He humbly accepted that he was not to enter Canaan. Now he has reached the great age of 120 and is about to step out of this remarkable story. It is time for him to commission the new leader.

Joshua caught Moses' eye early on in the journey. We met him first when he fought Amalek in the valley, and he, along with Caleb, was one of the spies who visited Canaan and came back speaking faith rather than fear. Moses clearly has confidence in him, although he recognises that even someone like Joshua can have his wobbly moments. So his parting message is simply, 'You have every reason to be courageous, because God is with you.' It is a message that God himself repeats, in Joshua 1:6–7, 9 and 18.

The wise old eyes of Moses look up from the pages of scripture to you and me, and the voice of that servant of God says to us, 'Be strong and courageous, for God is with you.'

When you feel afraid, remember Moses
and listen to his message of courage to you.

MICHAEL MITTON

Moses' final journey

Then Moses went up from the plains of Moab to Mount Nebo, to the top of Pisgah, which is opposite Jericho, and the Lord showed him the whole land… The Lord said to him, 'This is the land of which I swore to Abraham, to Isaac, and to Jacob, saying, "I will give it to your descendants"; I have let you see it with your eyes, but you shall not cross over there.' Then Moses, the servant of the Lord, died there in the land of Moab, at the Lord's command.

Moses comes to his final day on earth. At God's command (Deuteronomy 32:48–50) he climbs Mt Nebo, which is over 2500 feet high and stands to the east of the Jordan. Like Horeb, this mountain must be climbed on his own. 'Pisgah' is the Hebrew word for 'summit', and as he arrives at that high point, no doubt a little tired and breathless, he gets an excellent view of the land promised to Abraham, Isaac and Jacob. He can see the city of Jericho, and maybe, with his prophetic heart of foresight, he can even see clouds of dust around crumbling walls, with bold Joshua sounding the trumpet.

As his strength starts to fail him, he has one last conversation with the God who has led him on such a momentous journey. By this stage, Moses is fully resigned to the divine plan and, although he will not personally enter the land, his heart is for his people, not himself. He is at peace because he now knows that they will dwell in the land. The plans of God will be fulfilled. It has all been worthwhile.

Moses had a humble and generous heart, and he was prepared to give his life for something of which he would never be a part. As servants of God, we have to recognise that we may not see the fruits of our prayers and labours—but who knows what vistas we may be granted in our final hours on this earth?

'And they sing the song of Moses, the servant of God, and the song of the Lamb: "Great and amazing are your deeds, Lord God the Almighty!"'
(Revelation 15:3).

MICHAEL MITTON

Healing in Matthew's Gospel

Some time ago, a church leader asked what I did, so I began to explain a little of my role as Director of The Christian Healing Mission. At the very mention of the word 'healing', his strong response was, 'Don't talk to me about healing!' He then went on to explain that his wife had fallen seriously ill some time before, and although he and his church had prayed fervently for her healing, she had died. Naturally her death had caused many in the church to ask questions about the ministry of healing, the power (or otherwise) of prayer and even the nature of a 'loving' God.

Christian healing is a topic that can provoke strong reactions—either stunning testimonies to God's goodness or anguished questions about why God did not do what he was expected to do.

The studies that follow are all taken from Matthew's Gospel. Some of the stories of healing are repeated on several days so that we can really get to grips with them, whereas others are not mentioned at all in this series but are still well worth reading thoughtfully. I hope to encourage us all to reflect on our reaction to Jesus the healer. What makes it hard for us to accept this ministry? What are our expectations and can we change them? What is it fair to expect? How do we respond to the figure of Jesus the healer?

Yet my aim in writing these notes is not primarily to focus on healing. During my many years exploring the wonders and frustrations of the ministry of healing, I have developed an approach that is centred on helping people to become more aware of the presence of God with them. The reason for this is that as they encounter him, healing or some other sort of transformation often follows.

By the time we finish looking together at some of the stories of Jesus' healing in Matthew's Gospel, I hope that we will be able to take our eyes off the ministry of healing and instead feel a fresh impact of the amazing person of Jesus himself.

JOHN RYELAND

It's OK to ask

When Jesus came down from the mountainside, large crowds followed him. A man with leprosy came and knelt before him and said, 'Lord, if you are willing, you can make me clean.'

An assumption we can make about healing is that if God knows everything, he must know everything about us and what we are going through; so if he wants to heal us, he will.

There is, of course, truth in this. God does indeed know everything. Yet as we read through the accounts of Jesus healing the sick, we see that he was often responding to people who asked for help. Sometimes their condition was not obvious or their request was made on behalf of another person, but in this story it is likely that the man's leprosy was obvious. Nevertheless, it seems as if Jesus responds not just to what he sees, but to what is requested of him.

This raises an interesting question: how often did Jesus *not* respond to needs that he saw, because he was not asked? I suspect this is one of many questions to which we will never know the answer. We often consider personal requests to be the least important aspect of prayer—something we do only after we have praised God, made our confession and lifted other people's needs to him. Only then do we deem it right to bring our own needs to him. However, Jesus went to great lengths to emphasise the value in asking: 'Ask and it will be given to you' (Matthew 7:7); 'You may ask me for anything in my name, and I will do it' (John 14:14). The point is that it is OK to ask. In fact, we are encouraged to ask. There may well be people in worse situations than our own, and we may feel awkward or embarrassed about asking for things for ourselves, but this is not the point. The reason for doing it is that Jesus seems to respond to requests; it is something he encourages.

Jesus spoke to Bartimaeus and asked him,
'What do you want me to do for you?' (Mark 10:51)
He asks you the same question, so how will you reply? Be honest!

JOHN RYELAND

Jesus' willingness to heal

A man with leprosy came and knelt before him and said, 'Lord, if you are willing, you can make me clean.' Jesus reached out his hand and touched the man. 'I am willing,' he said. 'Be clean!' Immediately he was cleansed of his leprosy.

We may have no difficulty in believing that God could heal us or someone we know: after all, healing must be technically possible for God. Perhaps a more challenging question to consider is: what do we think is the chance of God healing us?

Many of us tend to link the likelihood of healing with our feelings about whether or not we deserve it. The trouble with this is that it is all too easy to think of many reasons why God would not heal us: we are not good enough, don't give enough, don't pray enough, and so on. However, such thoughts put the focus on ourselves; healing is seen as something for which we have to qualify, and few of us are qualified.

This story of the leper who was healed challenges this perception. The focus is not on the worthiness of the leper but, rather, on the willingness of Jesus. So one of the immediate questions that arises is this: if Jesus is so willing, why don't we see more healing? Perhaps, however, the question we should be asking is this: do I really believe that Jesus is willing to heal me?

Jesus' willingness to heal can be glimpsed in Galatians 2:20, where Paul writes about 'the Son of God, who loved me and gave himself for me'. Here Paul outlines the willingness of Jesus to give himself for us. This is taken a step further in Romans 8:32: 'He who did not spare his own Son, but gave him up for us all—how will he not also, along with him, graciously give us all things?'

There seems to be a real willingness on the part of Jesus, but can we believe it?

Do you find it hard to believe that Jesus wants to heal you?
If he was willing to give his life for you, and he has expressed
his willingness to heal, why might this be the case?

JOHN RYELAND

Taking Jesus seriously

Jesus reached out his hand and touched the man. 'I am willing,' he said. 'Be clean!' Immediately he was cleansed of his leprosy.

The authority of Jesus was amazing; he could speak a word and physical healing happened. So, if leprosy responded to his words immediately, how seriously do we take them? All too often we look at the promises of Jesus and file them under the 'too good to be true' heading.

One of Jesus' promises that challenges us as we think about the topic of healing can be found in John 10:10: 'I have come that they may have life, and have it to the full.' This verse appears quite a long way through a section that actually begins with the healing of a blind man at the beginning of John 9. Jesus healed the blind man, who was subsequently questioned by the Pharisees and thrown out of the synagogue. Jesus found him and spoke to him again, and then we discover the Pharisees rejoining the conversation. It is in this context, presumably with the man who had been healed standing by, that Jesus spoke the words promising fullness of life. How seriously do we take them?

This is one of the big challenges facing us as we ponder the healing stories of Jesus. Do we actually believe that it is his desire to heal us? Perhaps we are so used to seeing a lack of healing that it is his willingness to heal that we question? This is at the heart of Matthew's story about the man with leprosy. In fact, the leper's first words to Jesus are a question about his willingness to heal—and Jesus responds with an unequivocal 'I am willing.'

The willingness of Jesus to heal is an outworking of his mission to bring abundant life to the world. However, it is not just the world in general for which he is concerned, but for each of us personally.

---

*If you are sick—whether physically, emotionally or in any other way—
what do you believe God's will is for you?*

JOHN RYELAND

The cost of healing

Jesus reached out his hand and touched the man. 'I am willing,' he said. 'Be clean!'

It appears, from reading the healing stories, that Jesus brought healing to people in a variety of ways—by a touch, by a word, sometimes both and sometimes neither. In this story, he uses both.

In this simple detail from the story of Jesus healing the leper, we read that Jesus touched the man. It is interesting that he didn't touch him after he had been healed, but he actually touched him while there was still a risk of infection and when he himself would be rendered ceremonially 'unclean' by the act. We don't know whether Jesus actually needed to touch the leper for the healing to take place, or whether the command to be clean would have sufficed, but it is likely that his touch would have conveyed immense compassion to an untouchable man.

This act of touching the leper gives us a picture of the whole ministry of Jesus. His role as Saviour was not conducted from on high, sending bolts of power across a vast distance to those in need, like a superman figure swooping down to do amazing things. The reality of Jesus the healer is, I think, quite different. The salvation that Jesus wrought cost him dearly—ridicule, scorn, pain and ultimately death—and in this we see his utter commitment to it.

In his encounter with the leper, Jesus was willing to pay an enormous price for the man's healing, rendering himself unclean and risking contamination. In this one act he demonstrated the depth of his love and compassion. As we look at the wider picture of Jesus' ministry to us all, we see him risking everything for the sake of opening up for us the means of a whole new relationship with his Father, and the means of our total transformation.

As you turn to God with your needs, take a moment to ponder what he has already done to bring about your transformation. Jesus physically touched the leper, but his whole incarnation and death represent his touch for you. How do you react to this?

JOHN RYELAND

God's agenda

Some men brought to him a paralysed man, lying on a mat. When Jesus saw their faith, he said to the man, 'Take heart, son; your sins are forgiven.'

If we are honest, most of us have a list of things that we want God to do for us. However, this healing story opens up the possibility that God might have his own agenda about what he wants to do in our lives.

The man who was brought to Jesus in the story had an obvious and visible need, seen in the fact that he could not walk to Jesus on his own but had to be carried by others. So it is interesting that the first thing Jesus did was not to bring healing to his body, but to deal with something else entirely: he assured the man that his sins were forgiven.

It would be wrong to make the assumption that healing is dependent upon a time of confession and forgiveness of sins (although confession is never a bad thing), but this passage does raise the possibility that God's priority for us may not coincide with what we think is the most important need in our lives.

When we ponder the disappointment that many people feel about the healing ministry, this is probably one of the key issues we ought to consider. What else is God seeking to do in our lives? Prayer for healing is not about coercing God to do what we want; rather, it is a door that we open for him to do whatever he knows is best for us.

If we pray for someone and the result is not as we would choose, it may be worth exploring what else God might be doing in their life. After all, it's possible that he wants to touch something else entirely.

What might God want to do in your own life, as well as the lives of others? You may harbour a sense of disappointment about what God is not doing in response to some of your prayers, but instead begin to open your eyes to how he may be bringing his touch to another part of your life.

JOHN RYELAND

Lifting our eyes

While he was saying this, a synagogue leader came and knelt before him and said, 'My daughter has just died. But come and put your hand on her, and she will live.'

This story of the dead girl and her pleading father is easy to visualise. All his hopes and dreams for his daughter have been dashed at the moment of her death, but we also see him lifting his eyes above his tragic circumstances and looking to Jesus.

However much we think we trust God and believe in his ability to help and guide us, when faced with a problem our default position is often to focus on it so closely that it begins to consume us. In this story, such a reaction would be understandable, yet when we face far less serious issues, worry and anxiety seem to be our natural response.

The lesson we learn from this anxious father is clear: look to Jesus. We have no idea how the thought came to him; perhaps he had heard of Jesus and the wonderful things he had done, or maybe he had witnessed some of the healing miracles himself. Whatever the connection, his immediate thought was to look to Jesus, recognising that Jesus could help him.

So what does it mean to look to Jesus? This can be interpreted in a number of ways: for example, it might mean holding before ourselves, in reality or imagination, a picture of Jesus; reading a passage of scripture that speaks of the wonder of Jesus or dwelling on a hymn or worship song. Another approach that Christians have traditionally found helpful is to spend time each day repeating a phrase such as 'Lord Jesus Christ, have mercy on me.' The result of this practice is often that the words come back to mind throughout the day, helping to keep Jesus central in our thinking.

The details of the way we look to Jesus are secondary to the importance of doing something to deliberately turn away from our anxieties and focus on the one who is so much greater.

What are the issues concerning you at the moment? Somehow, turn your attention to Jesus and away from your anxiety. Reflect on the difference that such a shift of focus makes.

JOHN RYELAND

What are we expecting?

While he was saying this, a synagogue leader came and knelt before him and said, 'My daughter has just died. But come and put your hand on her, and she will live.' Jesus got up and went with him, and so did his disciples. Just then a woman who had been subject to bleeding for twelve years came up behind him and touched the edge of his cloak. She said to herself, 'If I only touch his cloak, I will be healed.' Jesus turned and saw her. 'Take heart, daughter,' he said, 'your faith has healed you.' And the woman was healed at that moment.

In our quest for healing, there are probably occasions when we would love to go right back to the time of Jesus and simply stand before him to receive healing. It all seems so simple as we read the Gospels! However, it was often far from simple, even then.

An interesting focus here is the synagogue leader's expectation. What was he expecting to happen and how were his expectations met? It is reasonable to assume that his request to Jesus summed up his expectations—that Jesus would come to his house, put his hand on the girl and cause life to return to her. It is likely that there was some sense of urgency about his request and that the sooner Jesus got there, the better.

Yet Matthew, Mark and Luke all link this story to the account of a woman who was suffering from bleeding. How frustrating it must have been when Jesus got waylaid by someone else! He was interrupted by this woman, so stopped and engaged with her. Why did Jesus not simply tell her to wait a while? He could have come back to her when he had attended to the girl. After all, she had been bleeding for twelve years, so surely another few minutes would not have made much difference.

Jesus was, of course, utterly unpredictable. Both parties were ultimately overjoyed at his ministry, although the girl's father certainly had to contend with a time of uncertainty as Jesus put his request aside to deal with another matter. We all know that Jesus has a wonderful heart, but I wonder how often we feel that his timing does not match our own.

What issues are you bringing to God? Is his response slower than you think it ought to be? Does his delay create chances for him to act in other ways?

JOHN RYELAND

Perseverance

Just then a woman who had been subject to bleeding for twelve years came up behind him and touched the edge of his cloak.

At what point do we give up pursuing healing and resign ourselves to learning to cope with the things that push us down? Some people may regard learning to cope as a form of healing in itself, but we certainly have no record of Jesus encouraging folk to accept their sicknesses and get on with life. The record of the Gospels is that all who came to him were healed.

The woman in this story had been pursuing healing for twelve years. In fact, Mark's account of the story reveals that she had pursued health to such an extent that she had spent all she had on doctors' fees. We don't know whether she reached out to Jesus as a result of desperation or out of genuine faith, but she certainly never gave up in her quest to find the good health that presumably she felt was her entitlement.

Is there a point at which we give up and accept that a situation is unlikely to change? There is certainly no obligation to pursue healing or, indeed, to expect others to do so, but there is something even more important that we should always doggedly pursue. The Bible reveals a God who seeks relationship with us. In fact, he pursues us relentlessly, as he longs for us to experience life in all its fullness. This is something that we need to take seriously. Whatever the conditions and afflictions that beset us, the mission of Jesus is that we have life in all its abundance, and from reading about the ministry of Jesus we discover that healing was a major part of the way he viewed abundant life.

Whether or not we choose to seek healing, we need to take seriously God's desire for us to have abundant life, and to ponder what that life may mean to us. Our pursuit of God should be ongoing and without end, as is his pursuit of us.

What does it mean for you that Jesus came to bring you abundant life? In what ways can you pursue what he is seeking to give you?

JOHN RYELAND

What does she have that I don't?

Just then a woman who had been subject to bleeding for twelve years came up behind him and touched the edge of his cloak. She said to herself, 'If I only touch his cloak, I will be healed.'

This story is a favourite for many people, possibly because there is something about the woman's action in touching Jesus' cloak that seems to connect with us. It is something that we all feel we would like to do—even if we don't know how. So what was so different about her?

The woman seemed to possess a unique blend of boldness with humility. She didn't simply stand at the back of the crowd with the attitude that God must know about her and therefore he would touch her if he wanted to, yet she didn't feel comfortable standing right in front of Jesus and demanding his attention either. She found a way of reaching out that was as bold as she dared to be, but it still took courage, effort and purpose. It was she, rather than the ones who were jostling for his attention, who was noticed and ultimately transformed.

How can we combine these qualities of boldness and humility in the way that we approach Jesus? There is certainly no need to march to the front during a church service and demand attention there and then, yet it may not be sufficient to remain at the back, hoping for God's touch without taking any action at all. The bleeding woman had come up with a plan to connect her need with Jesus' power, and we need to do likewise, even if it takes imagination and ingenuity to work out a personal approach to him.

It is not that we have to work for our healing, but we are required to make a response to the one who stands before us and offers us abundant life.

Slowly read through this story again and imagine yourself as the woman who touched Jesus' cloak. What is your equivalent to touching his cloak? What practical response can you see yourself making in the presence of Christ the healer?

JOHN RYELAND

What do I have to do to be healed?

She said to herself, 'If I only touch his cloak, I will be healed.'

It would be wonderful if there was a magic formula for getting healed. This ministry would be so much easier if we could guarantee that by saying the right words or doing the right thing, healing would happen naturally. In fact, one of the problems in listening to a testimony of healing is that it is easy to make the assumption that if we do exactly the same as that person did, the result must be the same. The trouble is that it doesn't work like this.

When we read the story of the woman with the flow of blood, we are not looking at someone who had a predetermined idea of the right way to approach Jesus. All we are told is that she had heard about him and decided to do something about it. It's unlikely that she had been told that the way to approach him was to creep up behind him and touch his cloak; the idea probably simply popped into her mind as a means of achieving the result that she wanted.

The encouraging message for us is that there appears to be no single correct way to approach Jesus for healing. When we hear of the lengths to which some people go in their quest for God, we need to recognise that this is their quest, not ours. We should not feel that we have to imitate other people in the way they approach God. It also means that we can be creative about approaching him, perhaps using art, poetry, shouting out loud or silent contemplation. As long as we are being ourselves and are connecting with Jesus, any method is fine. Each of us will approach him differently, but what matters to him is the heart that is seeking him, not the way we approach.

How do you best find the presence of Jesus—through times of prayer, Bible study, walking, a quiet atmosphere, writing or artistic expression? Be yourself as you seek to express your deepest needs to him.

JOHN RYELAND

Christ the healer

She said to herself, 'If I only touch his cloak, I will be healed.' Jesus turned and saw her.

When we read some of the biblical accounts of Jesus healing people, or hear testimonies of his healing people nowadays, we can be left with the impression that it only happens to specially chosen individuals. However, this account of a woman's healing puts the emphasis far more on Jesus as a reservoir of healing than on the choice he made to heal her in particular.

She approached Jesus and touched his cloak, and, as she did so, he turned and saw her. He certainly didn't pick her out of the crowd or make any conscious decision to reach out and heal her, and yet healing flowed out of him as a natural response to her act of faith. If this was true for her, why not for us?

Too often we feel that we are unlikely to qualify as candidates for divine healing, either because of past misdemeanours or because we do not feel that our present life is making enough impression on the world to justify a spectacular intervention by God. Yet if Jesus is a reservoir of healing, and not looking out for people qualified or righteous enough to be healed, why would he not be just such a reservoir for us?

Inevitably this raises all sorts of questions about why Jesus has not healed many people who have suffered greatly, and we have already touched upon the suggestion that God might have his own agenda or other ways in which he might want to bring transformation to us. However, the invitation is the same for us all: whoever we are and whatever we have done, we are welcome to come to Jesus, the fountain, the living water—and drink. It is not that some people are preselected to receive from him, but that he invites us all to take seriously the call to come to him.

Jesus is with you right now, where you are, so focus on his presence and bring your needs and requests to him with honesty and expectation.

JOHN RYELAND

The atmosphere for prayer

A man with a shrivelled hand was there. Looking for a reason to bring charges against Jesus, [the Pharisees] asked him, 'Is it lawful to heal on the Sabbath?'

If we think about arranging a healing service or a time for receiving personal prayer, most of us would probably choose to set it in an atmosphere of either praise and worship or quiet reflection. Not many would choose an atmosphere of accusation and conflict, but this is precisely the context for the story of the healing of the man with a shrivelled hand.

Despite all the scheming and plotting of the Pharisees, a man was wonderfully healed right before their eyes. This assures us that although we may rarely experience the perfect situation for an encounter with God, it does not mean that he cannot touch us. Healing is not about the atmosphere that surrounds us, or the worship or the quietness. It is, of course, all about the touch of Jesus.

This is such good news, regardless of whether we are coming to God for healing, for something else or for nothing at all. Our surroundings might affect us, even drawing our attention away from God, but it certainly does not mean that he is excluded from our lives. There may be something on our minds—a cross word we've had with someone, or a feeling that others are against us—and naturally we want to set right as much as we can, but none of these things can keep God away from us.

It largely comes down to a question of focus. If our focus is on ourselves and our past, then we are looking in the wrong direction. Similarly, if our focus is on the feeling in our surroundings, then our focus is misplaced. Our invitation is to take our eyes off everything that may get in the way and look to Jesus.

Think about the things going on in your life right now. How are you feeling? What issues are preoccupying you? How are they affecting your life with God, and is it possible to change your focus?

JOHN RYELAND

It's OK to be in need

[Jesus] said to them, 'If any of you has a sheep and it falls into a pit on the Sabbath, will you not take hold of it and lift it out?' How much more valuable is a person than a sheep! Therefore it is lawful to do good on the Sabbath.' Then he said to the man, 'Stretch out your hand.' So he stretched it out and it was completely restored, just as sound as the other.

One of the reassuring touches about the healing ministry of Jesus is that he takes all judgement out of sickness. If we are ill, it is easy to wonder, 'Why am I in this state?' Then it is only a small step to start looking at the suffering of others and question why they too are in their difficult situations.

In this story, Jesus draws an analogy between sickness and an animal that has fallen into a pit. We make no judgement about why the animal is in the pit. It may have fallen in by accident, been pushed in or wandered in, from idle curiosity; it doesn't matter. The sheep is in a pit and our natural reaction is to lift it out.

This is so liberating. We can be very quick to shine a spotlight upon ourselves: am I good enough to be healed? Have I done enough to earn the touch of God? Are there things I have to do first to persuade God to touch me?

The first step is simply to recognise that we are in a pit and that we need a Saviour to lift us out because we cannot do it ourselves. This is where healing begins—not with what we have to do, but in the recognition that we are powerless to help ourselves and we need his touch.

Reflect on some of the things you are tempted to do to facilitate the touch of Jesus in your life. Some of them may be excellent but others less helpful. Which will genuinely open the door for you to draw closer to him, and which are attempts to lift yourself out of the pit?

JOHN RYELAND

The naturalness of healing

He said to them, 'If any of you has a sheep and it falls into a pit on the Sabbath, will you not take hold of it and lift it out? How much more valuable is a person than a sheep! Therefore it is lawful to do good on the Sabbath.'

One of the great questions about healing, which we often wrestle with, is this: does God actually want to heal us? Could it be that God has sent the sickness to us and that somehow it will sow good into our lives? The words of Jesus as he looks at this man suffering with a withered hand challenge such thinking and give us something of God's perspective on sickness and healing.

Jesus has just been asked whether it is lawful to heal on the sabbath. The Pharisees are not interested in the question of healing itself, but are asking a technical question about the lawfulness of this ministry on a sabbath. In answering their question, Jesus pans out to present us with a wider picture of healing. He likens it to showing care to an unfortunate animal, and ends by reflecting on how much more valuable are people than sheep.

The Bible does not portray God as the designer of an obscure obstacle course through which we have to navigate, or as the creator of a precarious tightrope for us to walk as we try to balance the problem of evil. Instead, he is presented as a shepherd looking down with compassion at a sheep in a pit, and naturally stooping to lift the unfortunate animal out.

As we draw to the end of this series, Matthew brings us back to the basis of our hope in the healing ministry. In our pursuit of healing and our attempts to find the right answers, and in trying to make sense of why it may not happen, we often overlook our value to God. It is natural for God to want to do good for us because he loves us.

What difficulties do you have in accepting this picture of God, lovingly gazing down on you as you are stuck in a pit, and seeking to lift you out?

JOHN RYELAND

Songs of praise

'You cannot become my disciple without giving up everything you own'
(Luke 14:33, NLT).

Jesus offered us this challenge—that the threshold to the spiritual way is simplicity. He said not, 'You cannot be perfected as a disciple' but, 'You cannot even become a disciple' without giving up all your possessions. It's the prerequisite, the condition of beginning. Francis of Assisi required the same of the men who aspired to make common cause with him.

The way of faith can become densely cluttered with paraphernalia—chalices, statues, candles, books, lecterns, pulpits, electronic gadgetry, craft materials, puppets and worship resources of every kind.

I love hymnody not least because it lets me keep things simple. The verse form and the tune help me remember the words, so I don't need a book in my hands. I can take a hymn anywhere. In a prison cell or hospital bed, out in the garden or by the sea, along the paths of a daily walk, the words of a hymn will arise in my mind as a prayer. I hope that if my eyesight and cognitive function fail as I grow old, beloved hymns will still be my companions, as I have seen them accompany others all the way to the end of life. And the best hymns comprise a complete theological argument or a rounded prayer, or exploration of a theme of faith. Hymns offer one of the greatest aids there is to keeping faith alive, and I notice that although successful churches differ from each other in many respects, invariably they have a thriving music ministry. Put simply: hymns rock.

Inspired by the monastic tradition that has profoundly shaped my own spiritual practice, in my hymn choices I am following the hours of light that go round the day, from first waking until I lie down to rest.

Sweet is the work, my God, my King,
To praise thy name, give thanks and sing,
To show thy love by morning light,
And talk of all thy truths at night. (Isaac Watts, 1674–1748)

Ancient of Days, who sang the world into being with your
creative word, may your Holy Spirit sing in me as I raise my voice
to bless your holy name.

PENELOPE WILCOCK

Before dawn

Very early in the morning, while it was still dark, Jesus got up, left the house and went off to a solitary place, where he prayed. Simon and his companions went to look for him, and when they found him, they exclaimed: 'Everyone is looking for you!' Jesus replied, 'Let us go somewhere else—to the nearby villages—so that I can preach there also. That is why I have come.'

I like to get up early. I move around the house quietly before the rest of the household is awake and rising, making a cup of tea. I settle myself on the sofa opposite the big window that looks out on the great ash trees at the foot of the garden, and watch the birth of the new day. The beautiful light of dawn begins in a peaceful silver luminescence, blushing into rose and gold as the sun comes up over the rim of the horizon.

The opening chapters of Mark's Gospel show us Jesus in much demand—healing the sick, casting out demons, teaching and travelling. In this passage we see how he was needed from first light—and these were not casual needs. Then, as now, Jesus was people's only hope. Everyone was looking for him. He drew strength for the day in solitary early communion with his Father. In this at least, we are no different from Jesus: that silent resting in the presence of God's peace and mystery before the day begins can make all the difference to our experience of everyday life.

Thinking of the words of 1 Samuel 1:19, 'They rose up in the morning early, and worshipped before the Lord' (KJV), Charles Spurgeon wrote a hymn, little known and rarely sung, but very beautiful. I encourage you to look it up and read it all. Here are the first two verses:

Sweetly the holy hymn breaks on the morning air;
before the world with smoke is dim we meet to offer prayer.

While flowers are wet with dews, dew of our souls, descend:
ere yet the sun the day renews, O Lord, Thy Spirit send.

Lord of our lives, in whose hand all our days are held, may all our endeavours have their beginning in you.

PENELOPE WILCOCK

The Tenth Sunday after Trinity   127

Beautiful morning

Make it your aim to live a quiet life, to mind your own business, and to earn your own living… In this way you will win the respect of those who are not believers, and you will not have to depend on anyone for what you need.

When my mother was a girl, she grumbled about the morning tasks to her mother one day—the cats to be fed, the dog to be walked, the eggs to fetch in from the hen-house, not to mention the floor to be swept and the breakfast to make. Her mother listened in amazement, responding with the simple question, 'What would we do if we didn't have any work?'

Grandma spoke the truth. A purposeful life is surely one of the greatest blessings God can give us. Even if we are not clever, not strong, and have few resources at our disposal, to have made a contribution makes every day feel worthwhile.

G.A. Studdert Kennedy, that beloved army chaplain of World War I, wrote exquisite poetry. In his hymn often sung on Palm Sunday, he conveys a sense of eagerness and purpose in greeting a new morning:

> *Awake, awake to love and work!*
> *The lark is in the sky;*
> *The fields are wet with diamond dew;*
> *The worlds awake to cry*
> *Their blessings on the Lord of life,*
> *As He goes meekly by.*
>
> *Come, let thy voice be one with theirs,*
> *Shout with their shout of praise;*
> *See how the giant sun soars up,*
> *Great lord of years and days!*
> *So let the love of Jesus come*
> *And set thy soul ablaze.*

Thank you, dearest Lord, for the gift of a new day. Help me to serve you well in the hours ahead, in all my work seeking to please you; for you alone are my Master.

PENELOPE WILCOCK

Morning Eucharist

See what love the Father has given us, that we should be called children of God; and so we are. The reason why the world does not know us is that it did not know him. Beloved, we are God's children now; it does not yet appear what we shall be, but we know that when he appears we shall be like him, for we shall see him as he is.

My friend, reflecting with humility on his failures and shortcomings, said he thought it unrealistic to expect perfection of ourselves. We are wiser to continue with hope and perseverance in the right direction than to beat ourselves up for not having yet arrived where we hope to be. This makes sense to me. We already belong to God and believe in him, and this remains true even when our best efforts are disappointing, even those times when we let ourselves and our Master down.

The apostle Paul described our present capacity for experiencing God's presence as catching sight of puzzling reflections in a mirror. The certain hope hidden in our hearts is the conviction that, in the fullness of time, we shall see our Saviour face to face (see 1 Corinthians 13:12).

This doesn't mean that our daily work and earthly life are substandard or only second-best, just that the physical plane's limitations—even with all its beauty and magnificence—prevent us from fully realising the glory of heaven. But still, there are windows into God's glory, like the wonders of nature, human love and music, and the glimpses we discover in prayer. For many of us, the Eucharist especially offers a deeply moving and transformative experience, allowing us a peep into the throne room of the king. Horatius Bonar described Holy Communion in these terms:

Here, O my Lord, I see Thee face to face;
Here would I touch and handle things unseen;
Here grasp with firmer hand eternal grace,
And all my weariness upon Thee lean.

Holy and transcendent God, even though we are like children—easily tired, often bewildered and prone to making mistakes—you are the one we call Father; we put all our trust in you. Lead us, by your grace, safely home.

PENELOPE WILCOCK

Using energy effectively

Put on all the armour that God gives you, so that you will be able to stand up against the Devil's evil tricks. For we are not fighting against human beings but against the wicked spiritual forces in the heavenly world, the rulers, authorities, and cosmic powers of this dark age. So put on God's armour now! Then when the evil day comes, you will be able to resist the enemy's attacks; and after fighting to the end, you will still hold your ground.

The work of the day happens in a context. This sounds obvious, but I often forget to factor it in. What happens around me affects what is reasonable for me to attempt. Where I live on the coast, for example, the weather varies dramatically. I must wait for days of sunshine to weed the garden or hang out laundry. Again, I live in a busy household, so I get up early to write if I want quiet, and I pace myself for what the day contains so that my energy will take me through with patience and courtesy intact.

Anyone living an effective life prepares for each day realistically, setting boundaries, welcoming some influences and peaceably (but firmly) resisting others. We work with the natural world: many people feel their creativity surge at particular hours of the day or seasons of the year. To offer the best of ourselves, we consider our context.

Into it all, we invite the Spirit of God. This is vitally important. He is in us, he sees further than we do—and he has our back!

I bind unto myself today the strong name of the Trinity
By invocation of the same, the Three in One and One in Three,

I bind unto myself today the virtues of the starlit heaven,
The glorious sun's life-giving ray, the whiteness of the moon at even,
The flashing of the lightning free, the whirling wind's tempestuous shocks,
The stable earth, the deep salt sea around the old eternal rocks.
Patrick of Ireland (fourth century), trs. Cecil Frances Alexander (1889)

O God, you know me better than I know myself. Stay with me through the work of this whole day, so that I may bring the strength and peace of Christ to all I attempt and everyone I meet.

PENELOPE WILCOCK

Discovering God's presence

Stand ready, with truth as a belt tight around your waist, with righteousness as your breastplate, and as your shoes the readiness to announce the Good News of peace. At all times carry faith as a shield; for with it you will be able to put out all the burning arrows shot by the Evil One. And accept salvation as a helmet, and the word of God as the sword which the Spirit gives you. Do all this in prayer, asking for God's help. Pray on every occasion, as the Spirit leads. For this reason keep alert and never give up.

Everybody's contribution is important. There are no menial tasks, no mundane chores. The distinction between 'ordinary' and 'special' people is false. We may look up to doctors, with their authority and education, but the mortality rate rises when the dustmen go on strike! Every head-teacher knows how powerful is the influence of the caretaker.

The World War I poet Siegfried Sassoon urged, 'Let every separate soul with courage shine, a kneeling angel holding faith's front line.'

Regardless of the part we play in our neighbourhood, workplace or church, the key to illumination is our attitude. Even if our tasks are solitary, the love and prayer we bring to them shines forth. If we immerse our daily work in the humility and kindness of Christ, remembering to offer all to God—both problems and successes—we will have been faithful.

And God will surprise us; he is there waiting for us if we are ready to detect the signs of his presence, the fragrance of his love. When the going is hard, he will breathe life into us and work with us.

Teach me, my God and King, in all things thee to see,
and what I do in anything to do it as for thee.

A servant with this clause makes drudgery divine:
who sweeps a room, as for thy laws, makes that and the action fine.
George Herbert (1633)

Help me to find something of you, my Father, in all I encounter. Teach me to be present to the day's work in such a way as to anchor the light of heaven and reflect the glory of your love.

PENELOPE WILCOCK

The team of oxen

[Jesus said] 'Come to me, all you who are weary and burdened, and I will give you rest. Take my yoke upon you and learn from me, for I am gentle and humble in heart, and you will find rest for your souls. For my yoke is easy and my burden is light.'

As a child working alongside my mother at home, I'd be given the straight-forward tasks, like washing up or cleaning brass or peeling potatoes, while she undertook the complexities of difficult recipes and household management. When I became disheartened in my boring jobs, she'd say sympathetically, 'Plod on!'

Sometimes, when life and work feel hard and discouraging, I say it to myself still: 'Plod on!' But now I also understand the power of being yoked together with Jesus. I'm not just left to it by myself. He is the lead ox; we do everything together, and that makes all the difference.

Clara Scott, a late-19th-century music teacher in Iowa, knew about keeping her eyes fixed on Jesus, following his lead in her work. The task of teaching children the mysteries of composition and notation needs patience and can be noisy as well as discouraging, but Clara added a sweet new twist to the notion of perseverance, because she wrote this hymn in waltz time—not so much 'Plod on' as 'Keep dancing'. If music while you work helps things go with a swing, then make mine a praise song.

Whether you see him as the experienced animal in the team of oxen yoked to the plough, or as your partner on the dance floor, the important thing is to follow his lead and keep in step with him.

Open my eyes, that I may see glimpses of truth Thou hast for me;
Place in my hands the wonderful key that shall unclasp and set me free.
Silently now I wait for Thee, ready, my God, Thy will to see;
Open my eyes, illumine me, Spirit divine!

In all I attempt today, dear Jesus, may I have the humility to watch your every move and follow your wise lead. May I take pride in every endeavour, knowing you are working alongside me, my example and my strength.

PENELOPE WILCOCK

Take tea breaks

**'Stay awake, for you do not know on what day your Lord is coming…
Therefore you also must be ready, for the Son of Man is coming at an
hour you do not expect. Who then is the faithful and wise servant,
whom his master has set over his household, to give them their food at
the proper time? Blessed is that servant whom his master will find so
doing when he comes.'**

In the last days of my husband Bernard's life, I was both nursing him at
home and preparing in the coming month to step up from pastoral charge
of two churches to six. Knowing he would not be long with me, Bernard
said with his customary glare, 'Don't forget to take days off!'

I replied, 'How can I? There just isn't time.'

'Oh,' he said, crestfallen, knowing this to be true. He thought for a
moment, then added, 'Well, then—take tea breaks.'

A master-builder, Bernard knew that getting the best from a team of
workers includes giving them time to rest as well as urging them on.

I remember how, as a teenager starting work in a children's home, I
often felt drowsy in the afternoon as I sewed in name-tapes or tackled a
stack of ironing. A sit down with a hot cup of tea and a snack helped a lot.

In serving Christ, as in setting about daily work, it pays to be gentle
with our human reality and give ourselves adequate time for refreshment.
You can't stay alert if you don't take tea breaks. 'Work, rest and play' is an
enduring formula for effective living. We won't burn out if we maintain
that balance.

> *O for a closer walk with God, a calm and heavenly frame,*
> *A light to shine upon the road that leads me to the Lamb!*
>
> *Where is the blessedness I knew when first I sought the Lord?*
> *Where is the soul-refreshing view of Jesus and his Word?*
> William Cowper (1772)

---

*Lord Jesus, help me to serve you faithfully and sensibly today. Give me the
strength to work honestly, but also the wisdom to take enough time to
play and rest, so that I can give of my best for your glory.*

PENELOPE WILCOCK

Afternoon light

**About five in the afternoon he went out and found still others standing around. He asked them, 'Why have you been standing here all day long doing nothing?' 'Because no one has hired us,' they answered...
[Jesus said] 'As long as it is day, we must do the works of him who sent me.' Night is coming, when no one can work. While I am in the world, I am the light of the world.'**

It takes some people a long time to find their work in the world. I remember meeting a young man who loved to be outdoors. His life first started to go wrong when he let his father insist that, instead of following his heart, taking an open-air labourer's job, he should follow in Dad's footsteps and work in a bank. That path eventually took the lad into prison on a drugs charge. But all was not lost, because Jesus found and touched him. He started again, this time an honest life. On his release, he found work fitting windows—letting light stream in from the outdoors he loved, to people on the inside.

When you find the work you were born to do in this life, you discover that both the struggle and the joy inherent in it fit the kind of person you are. Although in every life journey there are hard and stony passes, those who find their true work can let their ordinary human light shine undimmed, as they were meant to do. And above and through it all comes streaming the heavenly light of God's love.

My God, I thank Thee, Who hast made the earth so bright;
So full of splendour and of joy, beauty and light;
So many glorious things are here, noble and right.

I thank Thee, too, that all our joy is touched with pain;
That shadows fall on brightest hours and thorns remain;
So that earth's bliss may be our guide and not our chain.
Adelaide Anne Procter (1825–64)

Employ me, O my Master, in the work of your kingdom—in your Light factory. May my light so shine in the world that people may see my good work and give glory to my Father in heaven.

PENELOPE WILCOCK

As the sun sets

For what we preach is not ourselves, but Jesus Christ as Lord, and ourselves as your servants for Jesus' sake. For God, who said, 'Let light shine out of darkness,' made his light shine in our hearts to give us the light of the knowledge of God's glory displayed in the face of Christ. But we have this treasure in jars of clay to show that this all-surpassing power is from God and not from us.

I believe everyone should have their time in the sun. When I read about farm animals living and dying cramped in crates under artificial lights, I feel desperate for them to be free.

My favourite photo of all time was of a small American mongrel. A number of us saw the Facebook post pleading, 'Help save lost dogs from euthanasia', and the sad, patient face looking through the concrete pen's iron bars. We crowd-funded his release from the pound into rescue, exulting when we made up the sum of money required.

Eventually came a photo of him setting off into the hopeful unknown. It was just a profile, pointy nose and perky ears seen through a porthole—the only passenger of a private jet, a few seats behind the pilot, travelling to his forever home. I'm glad that little dog had his time in the sun. I think it's how the Father meant things to be when he created heaven and earth. Rain, storm, flood, wind, thunder—we have all those—but there is many a sunny afternoon as we travel, saved and free, on our way to our forever home.

> *Hail, gladdening Light, of his pure glory poured,*
> *who is immortal Father, heavenly blest;*
> *Holiest of Holies, Jesus Christ our Lord!*
> *Now are we come to the sun's hour of rest;*
> *the lights of evening round us shine,*
> *we hymn the Father, Son and Holy Spirit divine.*
> *Translated from the Greek by John Keble (1834)*

Father, you made us for happiness. You love us. In our dealings with one another, may we reflect the kindness of the light of your countenance.

PENELOPE WILCOCK

Dusk

Let us, then, go to him outside the camp, bearing the disgrace he bore. For here we do not have an enduring city, but we are looking for the city that is to come. Through Jesus, therefore, let us continually offer to God a sacrifice of praise—the fruit of lips that openly profess his name. And do not forget to do good and to share with others, for with such sacrifices God is pleased.

Taking an average Englishwoman's life expectancy and thinking of a life as a week (starting on Monday), by now I must be in the early hours of Friday morning. Quite a sobering thought—time marching on!

The Hindu tradition sees life as divided into four stages—Student, Householder, Pilgrim and Ascetic. At about my age, it is time to gradually hand over worldly responsibilities to the next generation and begin to take seriously the contemplation of spiritual matters. My Pilgrim life-stage is beginning, a preparation for the asceticism of old age. Hindus call it 'going into the woods' (somewhat like 'going bush'), or, as the writer to the Hebrews puts it, going 'outside the camp' (v. 13).

In our hymn extract for today, I especially love the idea of a good friend being one who reminds me of the call of the gospel, should they have reason to think I have become too involved with the world's baubles and falsity. All life is holy, of course; reverence and faith belong to every age. It is a beautiful thing to teach a child to pray. But as life turns toward dusk, it's time to lay aside the tools of daylight hours. Evening is for gazing into the fire—reviewing the day, praying, giving thanks. But even dusk has its chores, of course: mine include feeding the fox!

Tell me the same old story, when you have cause to fear
That this world's empty glory is costing me too dear;
And when the Lord's bright glory is dawning on my soul,
Tell me the old, old story: 'Christ Jesus makes thee whole.'
Katherine Hankey (1866)

Holy One, though I am here in this world now, help me remember that it is not for ever. Help me to keep my sights on my destination, for I am travelling home to you.

PENELOPE WILCOCK

Closing down the house

I thank my God for you every time I think of you; and… I pray with joy because of the way in which you have helped me in the work of the gospel from the very first day until now. And so I am sure that God, who began this good work in you, will carry it on until it is finished on the Day of Christ Jesus. You are always in my heart!

On the wall of my room I have a beautiful calligraphy. I asked my daughter, an artist, to paint it for me. It says, 'Set your house in order.'

'Flylady', an internet adviser on things domestic, has many fans. She's very hot on leaving everything tidy and clean before going to bed—last thing, shine the sink (www.flylady.net).

Sir Francis Drake observed about our life's endeavours 'It is not the beginning, but the continuing of the same unto the end, until it be thoroughly finished, which yieldeth the true glory.' In so doing we follow the divine pattern: God promises to finish and fulfil his work of salvation in our souls.

I believe it is part of the courage of a Christian life that we accept responsibility, keeping and leaving in good order (or even improving) all that is entrusted into our hands. To achieve this not inconsiderable task, it helps if we keep a discipline of simplicity in both what we own and what we plan to do. We get in a muddle when we have and attempt too much.

Captain of Israel's host, and Guide of all who seek the land above,
Beneath Thy shadow we abide, the cloud of Thy protecting love;
Our strength, Thy grace; our rule, Thy Word; our end, the glory of the Lord.

By Thine unerring Spirit led, we shall not in the desert stray;
We shall not full direction need, nor miss our providential way;
As far from danger as from fear, while Love, almighty Love, is near.
Charles Wesley (1707–88)

May I stay close to you in everything, dear Master. May I fulfil responsibly the work you have entrusted to me and keep the faith you have revealed in my heart. May I be yours for ever.

PENELOPE WILCOCK

Going to sleep

I am now ready to be offered, and the time of my departure is at hand. I have fought a good fight, I have finished my course, I have kept the faith: henceforth there is laid up for me a crown of righteousness, which the Lord, the righteous judge, shall give me at that day: and not to me only, but unto all them also that love his appearing.

These words by novelist Pam Brown stopped me in my tracks: 'For every person who has ever lived there has come, at last, a spring he will never see. Glory then in the springs that are yours.'

'Yes,' said my heart. How precious the gift of life, every moment to be savoured—ours to fill with meaning and love.

Icon painters represent the soul as a child. So, in icons of the death of Mary, mother of Jesus, her adult form is seen on her deathbed, while Christ, flanked with angels, comes down to receive into his arms the trusting child of her soul. This is a wonderful insight of the circle made complete. He receives her who gave him earthly life into the eternal life that only he can give. This portrays death as it is—part of life, not its end. Birth and death balance one another; life is eternal. The original word that brought life into being—'Let there be light'—cannot be undone. The light shines on and the darkness will never put it out. Only in the sense of a homecoming is death our journey's end.

> *Lead, kindly light, amid the encircling gloom,*
> *Lead thou me on.*
> *The night is dark, and I am far from home;*
> *Lead thou me on.*
> *Keep thou my feet; I do not ask to see*
> *The distant scene, one step enough for me.*
> *John Henry Newman (1833)*

Thank you for the treasure and the wonder of this precious life you have given me, and the chance to love you. May I be faithful in this ordinary day. May I walk closely with you through all the days of my life, so that one day I will hear you say, 'Well done, good and faithful servant.' Into your hands, dear Master, I commend my spirit.

PENELOPE WILCOCK

Reading *New Daylight* in a group

SALLY WELCH

I am aware that although some of you cherish the moments of quiet during the day that enable you to read and reflect on the passages we offer you in *New Daylight*, other readers prefer to study in small groups, to enable conversation and discussion and the sharing of insights. With this in mind, here are some ideas for discussion starters within a study group. Some of the questions are generic and can be applied to any set of contributions within this issue; others are specific to certain sets of readings. I hope they generate some interesting reflections and conversations.

General discussion starters

These questions can be used for any study series within this issue. Remember, there are no right or wrong answers; they are intended simply to enable a group to engage in conversation.

- What do you think is the main idea or theme of the author in this series? Do you think the writer succeeded in communicating this idea to you, or were you more interested in the side issues?

- Have you had any experience of the issues that are raised in the study? How have they affected your life?

- What evidence does the author use to support their ideas? Do they use personal observations and experience, facts, or quotations from other authorities? Which appeals to you most?

- Does the author make a 'call to action'? Is that call realistic and achievable? Do you think their ideas will work in the secular world?

- Can you identify specific passages that struck you personally—as interesting, profound, difficult to understand or illuminating?

- Did you learn something new from reading this series? Will you think differently about some things, and if so, what are they?

Healing in Matthew's Gospel (John Ryeland)

- 'Praying for healing is not about coercing God to do what we want, but rather a door we open for him to do whatever he knows is best for us.' Do you agree?

- What is your definition of healing? Have you had any experiences of healing, either in your life or in the life of your community?

Hildegard of Bingen (Helen Julian CSF)

- If you can, look at Hildegard's illustrations (www.abtei-st-hildegard. de/?page_id=4721) or listen to her music (www.bbc.co.uk/music/ artists/2d923f7b-45a1-4204-beb8-5b106e913b58). Does this help you to understand her better?

- How important are music and art for you in worship?

Moving on with Joshua (John Twisleton)

- 'Joshua was old and advanced in years.' How has your faith changed as you have advanced in years? What is the role of older people in church communities today? How might it be changed and developed?

- Have there been times when you were aware of God working out his promises through you? How did it feel?

Reflective question: Music for the Journey

Penelope Wilcock shared with us the hymns that accompany her through the hours of the day. What hymns would you choose to support and sustain you for your daily routine?

Author profile: Peter Waddell

Peter Waddell is a new writer for *New Daylight*. Editor **Sally Welch** asked him to tell us a bit about himself and his work.

Can you tell us how long you have been an Anglican priest, and what first inspired you to seek ordination?

I have been ordained for 15 years, and what first inspired me was the sense that God means there will one day be justice. That, and the influence of a tremendous local parish priest.

You write in your biography that you spent eleven years in university chaplaincy. Can you describe what that involved?

Teaching theology, journeying with people as they grew up in every way, presenting the faith before sceptical audiences, dealing with pastoral crises, and drinking a phenomenal amount of coffee!

What were the best and worst things about your chaplaincy role?

The best: daily conversations about God with people who had nothing to do with the church. The worst: very occasionally having to bury students.

You are currently writing on 'Christianity, Judaism and the Holocaust'. How did you get interested in that?

It poses some of the sharpest questions. Why did God let it happen? Does intercessory prayer work? Can murderers be forgiven? To what extent was it the church's fault, and what might that mean for the truth of the gospel? I write to find out what I think.

Which spiritual writers have influenced you and in what ways?

Rowan Williams, Charles Gore, Philip Yancey, C.S. Lewis—they keep me Christian when sometimes it seems easier not to be. They hold head and heart together, they're never afraid to dive into the biggest questions, and they don't let themselves get distracted by trivia.

Do you have an unfulfilled wish or ambition?

I have finally accepted that being Northern Ireland goalkeeper is not going to happen.

One final question: what would you like your tombstone to say?

Dad. Husband. Preacher.

An extract from
Experiencing Christ's Love

In *Experiencing Christ's Love*, author John Twisleton reminds us of Jesus' gracious challenge to love God with heart, soul and mind, and to love our neighbour and ourselves. Against the backdrop of the message of God's unconditional love in Jesus Christ, he delivers a wake-up call to the basic Christian patterns of worship, prayer, study, service and reflection. The following extract is taken from the first chapter.

First love: worship

'You shall love the Lord your God with all your heart' (Matthew 22:37). I am intrigued by worship. It's been around since before the world was made and will continue after its predicted meltdown. There's something awesome about connecting the heart of the universe with the human heart and lifting hearts together towards what is ultimate. It's extravagant, lacks restraint and goes beyond reason in the way love is bound to do... In it we touch the face of God and something of him rubs off on us: 'Look to him and be radiant' (Psalm 34:5). When I was a teenager I found a remarkable place where Sunday services were like heaven to me. It was something totally different. The priest seemed like a saint and the unself-conscious ceremonial, music and preaching made heaven above real and brought radiance to faces around me. I sought and found a word in the dictionary that summed it up—'numinous' or filled with a sense of the supernatural, a sense that up to then I had not seen exercised.

Being so intrigued by worship, I'm writing this book partly as a call to recapture that sense of the supernatural which worship in the western church seems to have lost. As someone drawn to God by the supernatural in worship I can understand why church attendance is in decline when so much of what we call celebration feels so earthbound. To me, God has sameness, yes, but is also utterly different in his holiness. When I worship on Sunday I say, 'Holy, holy, holy, Lord, God of power and might' and expect to leave church different because of expectations of God, worship and the church raised all those years ago.

Suspicion of otherworldliness has grown on account of religious fanatics, unhinged through excessive irrationality, who see God as terrifyingly different, with the sameness to us who bear his image lost. Religion like money, power or sex is God-given but gets man-handled! The etymology of the word 'religion' is linked to the Latin *ligare*, meaning 'to bind'. I am unapologetically religious—regularly attending Sunday worship—because I want to keep re-binding myself to God and his people. So much of my life loosens me from what's ultimate, from the love of God. I need to continually bind myself back to God through the five loves Jesus describes in his summary of religion: '"You shall love the Lord your God with all your heart, and with all your soul, and with all your mind." This is the greatest and first commandment. And a second is like it: "You shall love your neighbour as yourself"' (Matthew 22:37–39)…

Experiencing Christ's love

How do you see God? Maybe he's close to you as a new Christian but the warmth of the first encounter is cooling. Or, like the mature Christians of Laodicea referred to in Revelation 3:16, 'you are lukewarm, and neither hot nor cold'. Either way, you are seeking to find strategies to know the love of God for real, inasmuch as it depends on you. The good news we'll come back to again and again is rooted in a vision of God who's 'always more ready to hear than we to pray and to give more than either we desire or deserve'. That lovely phrase from the Collect is read as part of worship day by day for a week every summer and, as with so many worship texts, acts to speak to us and remind us, as well as God, for whom all human worship is unnecessary reminder.

Like the Collect, this book is a reminder of love, being loved and loving, for which words matter less than attitudes and deeds, so the book is at heart a reminder to stick at loving God in the five aspects Jesus Christ invites, knowing 'we love because he first loved us' (1 John 4:19).

No one writes more eloquently about the love of God in Jesus Christ than the apostle Paul whose writings are a substantial part of the New Testament. Even his words, with all their force, crack as they address the love of God shown us in Jesus Christ. When, for example, Paul speaks to the Ephesians of 'knowing the love of Christ which passes knowledge', what does he mean? There's real ambiguity about the phrase 'knowing the love of Christ' and it's helpful to examine it.

Does Paul mean God's love for us? Or the blessings that come from our loving God? Or is it God's love in Christ for all that is, that he draws us into?

These are three ways of interpreting that phrase 'knowing the love of Christ' and they are all precious insights. To know the Son of God loved us and gave himself for us is, as Paul puts it in Galatians 2:20, our greatest motivator. To love God in the face of Jesus Christ is a blessing, since our devotion to him is God's gift passing earthly knowledge, and as Jesus himself says in Matthew 5:6, wanting most of all what God wants will satisfy us fully. To know the love of Christ, thirdly, is to sympathise with and enter into God's compassion towards all people and all things, shown in the perpetual gift of his Son Jesus Christ.

I don't know which of the three interpretations of 'knowing the love of Christ' is right—it's probably all three! We'll follow them chapter by chapter as variations on a theme: downward love for us from God, upward love from us to him and outward love from God and believers to the world. Whatever Paul meant by 'knowing the love of Christ which passes knowledge', I want that love, from him, for him and with him and I would that were so for all of us and for the whole creation.

Christianity starts with God's love for us in Christ, and our response follows, a disciplined response which bears fruit in bringing others to experience Christ's love. That response is corporate, a receiving and giving out, with all followers of Jesus in this world and the next. It is corporate because the many-sided love of God can only be grasped 'with all the saints' (Ephesians 3:18). This truth is captured eloquently by Baron Friedrich von Hügel when he writes of the Christian calling to become 'a great living cloth of gold with not only the woof going from God to man [sic] and from man to God, but also the warp going from man to man… and thus the primary and full Bride of Christ never is, nor can be, the individual man at prayer, but only this complete organism of all the faithful people throughout time and space'… When I go to church I go to worship and engage with God in Christ, present in bread and wine, in preaching, prayer and fellowship. Sometimes the sermon's dull, the sacrament feels empty or the prayers sound flat. One way or another—and it's good there are a number of ways—Christ makes his presence real to me. Sometimes it's in a conversation or kind action I experience afterwards involving a fellow Christian. That reminds me that my commitment to worship isn't just as an individual but is part of something much bigger, that 'great living cloth of gold' which is the church, the 'complete organism of all the faithful people throughout space and time'.

John Twisleton is a Sussex priest, theologian and pastor. He broadcasts regularly on Premier Radio. To order a copy of his book, please visit brfonline.org.uk or use the order form on page 149.

Bible readings for special times

Facing Death
Rachel Boulding

This collection of 18 undated reflections, originally published in *New Daylight* Bible reading notes, draws encouragement and comfort from the Bible and from the author's own experience for those going through life-limiting illness and for their family and carers. With moving vulnerability and without denying the difficult reality of the situation, Rachel Boulding suggests a way to confront terminal illness with faith and hope in a loving God.

Facing Death
Rachel Boulding
978 0 85746 564 1 £3.99
brfonline.org.uk

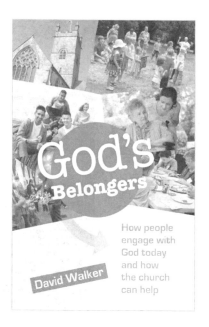

God's Belongers should transform our thinking about what it means to belong to church. David Walker offers a fourfold model of belonging: through relationship, through place, through events, and through activities. He shows how 'belonging' can encompass a far wider group of people than those who attend weekly services, opening up creative opportunities for mission in today's world.

God's Belongers
How people engage with God today and how the church can help
David Walker
978 0 85746 467 5 £8.99
brfonline.org.uk

Combining missional vision with practical advice, these resources, written by Laura Treneer, give you the tools you need to transform your church communications. Ideal for church teams who want to reach their communities effectively, and a perfect gift for church leaders and volunteers who are short on time but need fast relevant advice.

Church Online: Websites
978 0 85746 552 8 £3.99

Church Online: Social media
978 0 85746 557 3 £3.99

Church from the Outside
978 0 85746 553 5 £3.99

Church from the Inside
978 0 85746 554 2 £3.99

brfonline.org.uk

To order

Online: brfonline.org.uk
Telephone: +44 (0)1865 319700
Mon–Fri 9.15–17.30

Delivery times within the UK are normally
15 working days. Prices are correct at the time of
going to press but may change without prior notice.

Title	Price	Qty	Total
Thinking of You	£9.99		
Outdoor Church	£9.99		
Edible Bible Crafts	£11.99		
Experiencing God's Love	£7.99		
Facing Death	£3.99		
God's Belongers	£8.99		
Church Online: Websites	£3.99		
Church Online: Social media	£3.99		
Church from the Outside: Displays, noticeboards, invitations, PR	£3.99		
Church from the Inside: Welcome, news sheets, magazines, stories	£3.99		

POSTAGE AND PACKING CHARGES			
Order value	UK	Europe	Rest of world
Under £7.00	£1.25	£3.00	£5.50
£7.00–£29.99	£2.25	£5.50	£10.00
£30.00 and over	FREE	Prices on request	

Total value of books	
Postage and packing	
Total for this order	

Please complete in BLOCK CAPITALS

Title .... First name/initials .... Surname ....

Address ....

.... Postcode ....

Acc. No. .... Telephone ....

Email ....

Please keep me informed about BRF's books and resources ☐ by email ☐ by post
Please keep me informed about the wider work of BRF ☐ by email ☐ by post

Method of payment

☐ Cheque (made payable to BRF)   ☐ MasterCard / Visa

Card no. [ ][ ][ ][ ] [ ][ ][ ][ ] [ ][ ][ ][ ] [ ][ ][ ][ ]

Valid from [ ][ ] [ ][ ]   Expires [ ][ ] [ ][ ]   Security code* [ ][ ][ ]

Last 3 digits on the reverse of the card

Signature* .... Date .... /............ /............

*ESSENTIAL IN ORDER TO PROCESS YOUR ORDER

Please return this form to: BRF, 15 The Chambers, Vineyard, Abingdon OX14 3FE | enquiries@brf.org.uk
To read our terms and find out about cancelling your order, please visit **brfonline.org.uk/terms**.

The Bible Reading Fellowship (BRF) is a Registered Charity (233280)

How to encourage Bible reading in your church

The Bible Reading Fellowship has been helping individuals connect with the Bible for over 90 years. We want to support churches as they seek to encourage church members into regular Bible reading.

Order a Bible reading resources pack

This pack is designed to give your church the tools to publicise our Bible reading notes. It includes:

- Sample Bible reading notes for your congregation to try.
- Publicity resources, including a poster.
- A church magazine feature about Bible reading notes.

The pack is free, but we welcome a £5 donation to cover the cost of postage. If you require a pack to be sent outside the UK or require a specific number of sample Bible reading notes, please contact us for postage costs. More information about what the current pack contains is available on our website.

How to order and find out more

- Visit **biblereadingnotes.org.uk/for-churches**
- Telephone BRF on +44 (0)1865 319700 Mon–Fri 9.15–17.30
- Write to us at BRF, 15 The Chambers, Vineyard, Abingdon OX14 3FE

Keep informed about our latest initiatives

We are continuing to develop resources to help churches encourage people into regular Bible reading, wherever they are on their journey. Join our email list at **biblereadingnotes.org.uk/helpingchurches** to stay informed about the latest initiatives that your church could benefit from.

Introduce a friend to our notes

We can send information about our notes and current prices for you to pass on. Please contact us.

Transforming Lives and Communities

The Bible Reading Fellowship is a charity that is passionate about making a difference through the Christian faith. We want to see lives and communities transformed through our creative programmes and resources for individuals, churches and schools. We are doing this by resourcing:

- **Christian growth and understanding of the Bible.** Through our Bible reading notes, books, digital resources, Quiet Days and other events, we're resourcing individuals, groups and leaders in churches for their own spiritual journey and for their ministry.

- **Church outreach in the local community.** BRF is the home of three programmes that churches are embracing to great effect as they seek to engage with their local communities: Messy Church, Who Let The Dads Out? and The Gift of Years.

- **Teaching Christianity in primary schools.** Our Barnabas in Schools team is working with primary-aged children and their teachers, enabling them to explore Christianity creatively and confidently within the school curriculum.

- **Children's and family ministry.** Through our Barnabas in Churches and Faith in Homes websites and published resources, we're working with churches and families, enabling children under 11, and the adults working with them, to explore Christianity creatively and bring the Bible alive.

Do you share our vision?

Sales of our books and Bible reading notes cover the cost of producing them. However, our other programmes are funded primarily by donations, grants and legacies. If you share our vision, would you help us to transform even more lives and communities? Your prayers and financial support are vital for the work that we do.

- You could support BRF's ministry with a one-off gift or regular donation (using the response form on page 153).

- You could consider making a bequest to BRF in your will (page 152).

- You could encourage your church to support BRF as part of your church's giving to home mission—perhaps focusing on a specific area of our ministry, or a particular member of our Barnabas team.

- Most important of all, you could support BRF with your prayers.

Make a lasting difference through a gift in your will

For almost a century The Bible Reading Fellowship (BRF) has been able to do amazing things thanks to the generosity of those who have supported us through gifts in wills. Today our creative programmes impact the lives of thousands of individuals across the UK and overseas.

One such programme is The Gift of Years, which aims to improve the spiritual lives of older people across the UK. Through local churches we are growing a network of Anna Chaplains who deliver spiritual care services to older people of strong, little or no faith.

The late Joyce Barrett was visited regularly by Anna Chaplains at her care home in Hampshire. Joyce often shared stories from her life and, over time, showed an openness and willingness to explore life's big questions. On one occasion an Anna Chaplain was delivering a Communion service at her care home. This sparked a conversation that would result in Joyce becoming a Christian at the age of 89.

Standing alongside teenagers at her baptism service, Joyce was, and still is, a powerful witness to the fact that it's never too late to follow Christ. When Joyce died a few months later, all three Anna Chaplains who had cared for her took part in service of thanksgiving for her life.

If you share our passion for making a difference through the Christian faith, please consider leaving a gift in your will to BRF. Gifts in wills are an important source of income for us and they don't need to be huge to make a real difference. For every £1 we receive, we invest 95p back into charitable activities. Just imagine what we could do over the next century with your help.

For further information about making a gift to BRF in your will, please visit **brf.org.uk** or contact Sophie on +44 (0)1865 319700 or email giving@brf.org.uk.

Whatever you can do or give, we thank you for your support.

SHARING OUR VISION—MAKING A GIFT

I would like to make a gift to support BRF. Please use my gift for:

☐ where it is needed most ☐ Barnabas Children's Ministry
☐ Messy Church ☐ Who Let The Dads Out? ☐ The Gift of Years

Title	First name/initials	Surname

Address

Postcode

Email

Telephone

Signature   Date

giftaid it   You can add an extra 25p to every £1 you give.

Please treat as Gift Aid donations all qualifying gifts of money made

☐ today,   ☐ in the past four years,   ☐ and in the future.

I am a UK taxpayer and understand that if I pay less Income Tax and/or Capital Gains Tax in the current tax year than the amount of Gift Aid claimed on all my donations, it is my responsibility to pay any difference.

☐ My donation does not qualify for Gift Aid.

Please notify BRF if you want to cancel this Gift Aid declaration, change your name or home address, or no longer pay sufficient tax on your income and/or capital gains.

Please complete other side of form ➲

Please return this form to:
BRF, 15 The Chambers, Vineyard, Abingdon OX14 3FE

BRF

The Bible Reading Fellowship is a Registered Charity (233280)

Regular giving

By Direct Debit:

☐ I would like to make a regular gift of £ _____ per month/quarter/year.
   Please also complete the Direct Debit instruction on page 159.

By Standing Order:

Please contact Priscilla Kew, tel. +44 (0)1235 462305; giving@brf.org.uk

One-off donation

Please accept my gift of:

☐ £10 ☐ £50 ☐ £100 Other £ _____

by (delete as appropriate):

☐ Cheque/Charity Voucher payable to 'BRF'

☐ MasterCard/Visa/Debit card/Charity card

Name on card

Card no. ☐☐☐☐ ☐☐☐☐ ☐☐☐☐ ☐☐☐☐

Valid from ☐☐ ☐☐   Expires ☐☐ ☐☐

Security code* ☐☐☐   *Last 3 digits on the reverse of the card
ESSENTIAL IN ORDER TO PROCESS YOUR PAYMENT

Signature   Date

We like to acknowledge all donations. However, if you do not wish to receive an acknowledgement, please tick here ☐

☞ Please complete other side of form

Please return this form to:
BRF, 15 The Chambers, Vineyard, Abingdon OX14 3FE

NEW DAYLIGHT SUBSCRIPTION RATES

Please note our subscription rates, current until April 2018:

Individual subscriptions
covering 3 issues for under 5 copies, payable in advance
(including postage & packing):

	UK	Europe	Rest of world
New Daylight	£16.50	£24.60	£28.50
New Daylight 3-year subscription (9 issues) (not available for Deluxe)	£45.00	N/A	N/A
New Daylight Deluxe per set of 3 issues p.a.	£20.85	£33.45	£40.50

Group subscriptions
covering 3 issues for 5 copies or more, sent to **one** UK address (post free):

New Daylight	£13.20 per set of 3 issues p.a.
New Daylight Deluxe	£16.95 per set of 3 issues p.a.

Please note that the annual billing period for group subscriptions runs from 1 May to 30 April.

Overseas group subscription rates
Available on request. Please email enquiries@brf.org.uk.

Copies may also be obtained from Christian bookshops:

New Daylight	£4.40 per copy
New Daylight Deluxe	£5.65 per copy

All our Bible reading notes can be ordered online by visiting
biblereadingnotes.org.uk/subscriptions

For information about our other Bible reading notes,
and apps for iPhone and iPod touch, visit
biblereadingnotes.org.uk

NEW DAYLIGHT INDIVIDUAL SUBSCRIPTION FORM

All our Bible reading notes can be ordered online by visiting
biblereadingnotes.org.uk/subscriptions

☐ I would like to take out a subscription:

Title .... First name/initials .... Surname ....

Address ....

.... Postcode ....

Telephone .... Email ....

Please send *New Daylight* beginning with the September 2017 / January 2018 / May 2018 issue (*delete as appropriate*):

(please tick box)	UK	Europe	Rest of world
New Daylight	☐ £16.50	☐ £24.60	☐ £28.50
New Daylight 3-year subscription	☐ £45.00	N/A	N/A
New Daylight Deluxe	☐ £20.85	☐ £33.45	☐ £40.50

Total enclosed £ .... (cheques should be made payable to 'BRF')

Please charge my MasterCard / Visa ☐ Debit card ☐ with £ ....

Card no. ☐☐☐☐ ☐☐☐☐ ☐☐☐☐ ☐☐☐☐

Valid from ☐☐☐☐ Expires ☐☐☐☐ Security code* ☐☐☐

Last 3 digits on the reverse of the card

Signature* .... Date ...... /...... /......

*ESSENTIAL IN ORDER TO PROCESS YOUR PAYMENT

To set up a Direct Debit, please also complete the Direct Debit instruction on page 159 and return it to BRF with this form.

Please return this form with the appropriate payment to:
BRF, 15 The Chambers, Vineyard, Abingdon OX14 3FE

To read our terms and find out about cancelling your order, please visit **brfonline.org.uk/terms**.

The Bible Reading Fellowship is a Registered Charity (233280)

ND0217

NEW DAYLIGHT GIFT SUBSCRIPTION FORM

☐ I would like to give a gift subscription (please provide both names and addresses):

Title .... First name/initials .... Surname ....

Address ....

.... Postcode ....

Telephone .... Email ....

Gift subscription name ....

Gift subscription address ....

.... Postcode ....

Gift message (20 words max. or include your own gift card):

....

....

Please send *New Daylight* beginning with the September 2017 / January 2018 / May 2018 issue (*delete as appropriate*):

(please tick box)	UK	Europe	Rest of world
New Daylight	☐ £16.50	☐ £24.60	☐ £28.50
New Daylight 3-year subscription	☐ £45.00	N/A	N/A
New Daylight Deluxe	☐ £20.85	☐ £33.45	☐ £40.50

Total enclosed £ .... (cheques should be made payable to 'BRF')

Please charge my MasterCard / Visa ☐ Debit card ☐ with £ ....

Card no. ☐☐☐☐ ☐☐☐☐ ☐☐☐☐ ☐☐☐☐

Valid from ☐☐ ☐☐   Expires ☐☐ ☐☐   Security code* ☐☐☐

Last 3 digits on the reverse of the card

Signature* .... Date ...... /...... /......

*ESSENTIAL IN ORDER TO PROCESS YOUR PAYMENT

To set up a Direct Debit, please also complete the Direct Debit instruction on page 159 and return it to BRF with this form.

Please return this form with the appropriate payment to:
BRF, 15 The Chambers, Vineyard, Abingdon OX14 3FE

To read our terms and find out about cancelling your order, please visit **brfonline.org.uk/terms**.

The Bible Reading Fellowship is a Registered Charity (233280)

You can pay for your annual subscription to our Bible reading notes using Direct Debit. You need only give your bank details once, and the payment is made automatically every year until you cancel it. If you would like to pay by Direct Debit, please use the form opposite, entering your BRF account number under 'Reference number'.

You are fully covered by the Direct Debit Guarantee:

The Direct Debit Guarantee

- This Guarantee is offered by all banks and building societies that accept instructions to pay Direct Debits.

- If there are any changes to the amount, date or frequency of your Direct Debit, The Bible Reading Fellowship will notify you 10 working days in advance of your account being debited or as otherwise agreed. If you request The Bible Reading Fellowship to collect a payment, confirmation of the amount and date will be given to you at the time of the request.

- If an error is made in the payment of your Direct Debit, by The Bible Reading Fellowship or your bank or building society, you are entitled to a full and immediate refund of the amount paid from your bank or building society.

- If you receive a refund you are not entitled to, you must pay it back when The Bible Reading Fellowship asks you to.

- You can cancel a Direct Debit at any time by simply contacting your bank or building society. Written confirmation may be required. Please also notify us.

The Bible Reading Fellowship

Instruction to your bank or building society to pay by Direct Debit

Please fill in the whole form using a ballpoint pen and return it to:
BRF, 15 The Chambers, Vineyard, Abingdon OX14 3FE

Service User Number: | 5 | 5 | 8 | 2 | 2 | 9 |

Name and full postal address of your bank or building society

To: The Manager	Bank/Building Society
Address	
	Postcode

Name(s) of account holder(s)

Branch sort code

| | | – | | | – | | | |

Bank/Building Society account number

| | | | | | | | | | |

Reference number

| | | | | | | | |

Instruction to your Bank/Building Society
Please pay The Bible Reading Fellowship Direct Debits from the account detailed in this instruction, subject to the safeguards assured by the Direct Debit Guarantee. I understand that this instruction may remain with The Bible Reading Fellowship and, if so, details will be passed electronically to my bank/building society.

Signature(s)

Banks and Building Societies may not accept Direct Debit instructions for some types of account.

This page is left blank for your notes.